the Idea of the Laity

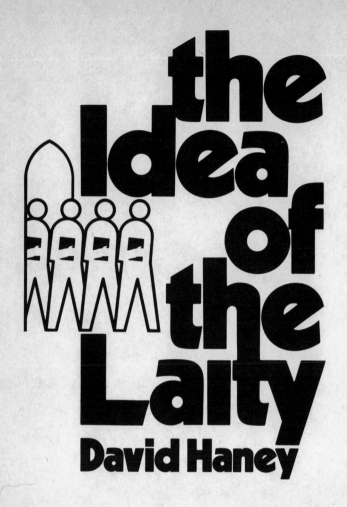

the Idea of the Laity

David Haney

ZONDERVAN
PUBLISHING HOUSE OF THE ZONDERVAN CORPORATION
GRAND RAPIDS, MICHIGAN 49506

To
AILEEN
and the kids
KAREN
STEVEN
PHILIP

Acknowledgments

We are grateful for the permission given us to quote from the following books and Bible translations:

Good News for Modern Man, the Today's English Version of the New Testament, copyrighted 1966 by the American Bible Society, New York, New York.

The New English Bible, New Testament. © 1961, 1970 by the Delegates of the Oxford University Press and the syndics of the Cambridge University Press. Reprinted by permission.

The New Testament in Modern English, translated by J. B. Phillips, copyrighted 1958. Reprinted by permission of the Macmillan Company, New York, and Geoffrey Bless, Ltd., London.

The Revised Standard Version, copyright © 1946, 1952 by Division of Christian Education of the National Council of Churches of Christ in the United States of America. Used by permission of the Division of Christian Education, National Council of Churches. Zondervan Publishing House, Licensee.

Amy Carmichael, *Edges of His Ways.* Copyright by The Society for Promoting Christian Knowledge, London.

Contents

Foreword

Among those evangelicals destined to be recognized as pioneers in the field of church renewal is . . . David Haney! This, his second book, [1] has been shaped more by experience than by mere theory. In his relationship with the Heritage Baptist Church of Annapolis, Maryland, he has become a living parable — a pastor who functions as a "player-coach" rather than as a "star quarterback." The practical suggestions in this volume reveal the fact that he is personally creative, spiritually sensitive — and practical! The fact that he is actually pastoring a congregation which is moving from old wine skins to new, constantly testing instead of talking, makes this book significant. For too long our books on renewal have been written by armchair generals who are not actually in danger of being wounded doing battle.

Someone has said, "No army can withstand an idea when its time has come." The life-style described in *The Idea of the Laity* is emerging across the nation. Small-group ministries, radical changes in Christian education, rethinking the use of church buildings, and Spirit-filled evangelism are among the areas also being tried by the People Who Care in Houston. [2] Readers of the pages which follow may well find themselves wondering, as I did, if David Haney had not been peeking over their shoulders, observing renewal in their own home towns and anticipating their needs.

This is the exciting moment! Those of us in renewal are discovering each other — and are discovering the same Holy Spirit breathing His life into us with a universal pat-

[1] David P. Haney. *Renew My Church.* (Grand Rapids: Zondervan Publishing House, 1972).

[2] Ralph W. Neighbour, Jr. *The Seven Last Words of the Church.* (Grand Rapids: Zondervan Publishing House, 1973).

tern. *What a time to be alive* — a time when His leadership is obviously manifesting itself in a new way within the body of the church!

Do what I did as you read this book: read it first to be inspired. Then search it again for those new ideas which can be implemented in the context of your own world. Finally, find a time to pray for others who have not yet found the way into the world of Spirit-led church life. They need our prayers!

RALPH W. NEIGHBOUR, JR.

Evangelism Research Foundation
Houston, Texas

Introduction

> *The Church must be forever building, for it is forever decaying. . . .*   T. S. ELIOT

"I bet my ministry" is a familiar expression to the congregation of the Heritage Baptist Church; I use it frequently when the underbrush has been cleared away enough to reveal a new and beckoning path. By it I mean my seriousness and my promise to stay by it and with it. To my continual delight, my people have always bet with me — not on me, but with me — and our travels, stumbles, and discoveries together over these five years-plus have never failed to keep us happy pilgrims. Thus, when I say "I bet my ministry" on *The Idea of the Laity*, the reader will know what is meant and the spirit in which it is said. In truth, to follow Christ is never a gamble, but it always calls for the wagering of our faith that Christ is always right.

The book is divided into ideas on *The Idea of the Laity*. The first three chapters are *ideas which have used me* for the past several years; the remaining chapters are *ideas which I have used* — and there is a difference! In a sense Chapters One through Three are theoretical; they seek to provide a perspective from which the Church and the laity are to be viewed. Chapters Four through Thirteen are intended to be practical.

The format of the book is designed for group study. There are thirteen chapters with accompanying Bible study passages to provide a quarter of study within the church program. The format may also be used in small-group or retreat settings. Its purpose is to get some ideas out in the open for group discussion and adaptation. Even to disagree or to improve upon the ideas fulfills my purpose! My only request and desire, as my neighbor Bill Andahazy says it, is for you to "have at it."

Renewal is neither a movement nor a fad. It is an *idea*. It is a faith wager that the needed renewal of the Church today will come only as the *laity become ministers* and the *pastors become equippers* of the ministers. Its glory is that it transcends all of our former divisions in the church: theological, methodological, sociological, denominational, and educational. Renewal fits the liberal and the conservative, the activist and the pietist, the lower class and the higher class, the Nazarene and the Catholic, the educated and the uneducated. It fits them all because it transcends them all; it has nothing to do with them, yet it has everything to do with them— for it alone seems to unify us. The renewal ideas and the widespread, spontaneous renewal groups simply contain all of us! This is true because renewal rightly ignores and sidesteps our artificially imposed barriers and focuses on "getting on with it" rather than "getting at it" with each other. True Christian unity allows us to keep our boundary markers, but it forces us to tear down our fences: there is too much to do, more than any of us can do alone, and it recognizes that there are too few of us to do it anyhow. Perhaps our patchwork quilt of divisions can be a thing of beauty after all, if it is held together by a common thread: our common task to "salt" and "light" this world in obedience to Christ and in the power of the Spirit. Renewal simply suggests that each of us has a ministry which is a part of the whole and, in turn, it asks us to help each other with those ministries.

Indebtedness is an integral part of any writing venture, and such is the case with *The Idea of the Laity*. Alton McEachern is right when he says that the only original thing about any of us is Original Sin! Any honest list of debtors would be too long to write or to read. There are some, however, of whom it must be said, "Without whom . . ."

For me, that list begins with my wife Aileen and our children, Karen, Steven, and Philip to whom this book is appropriately and affectionately dedicated. Next are my secretary, Joan Myers, and then my associate, Willard G. Wild. Both of their workloads double when I pick up the pen, and both of them do it with a grace which leads me to think they really don't mind. Special thanks is due Willard Wild for his assistance with the discussion questions for the various chapters.

With the exception of Chapter Thirteen, there are no untried ideas in this book. Since it was written for lay men and women, I gave our Yokefellow groups and the congregation at Heritage Church "veto powers" in open discussion and congregational dialogues. They exercised that power on several chapters in particular. Chapter Three was rewritten by our Yokefellow Two group, Chapter Four by the Yokefellow One group, and Chapters Seven, Eight, Ten, and Twelve by the congregation-at-large in a series of Sunday night dialogues. Gratitude must also be expressed to other churches and groups who have allowed me to share these ideas: the First Baptist Churches of Springfield, Georgia and Charles Town, West Virginia; the Quaker Hill Conference Center (Society of Friends), Richmond, Indiana; and the Evangelism Research Foundation Seminar, Chateau d'Oex, Switzerland.

Of a different sort are eight men who not only serve as anvils for my ideas, but frequently as hammers, too; they have never ceased to encourage me to "Write!" at our every encounter. I would sooner die than face their frowns and, hence, another book! They are Elton Trueblood, Carl F. H. Henry, Ralph Neighbour, Jr., James Mahoney, R. G. Puckett, Michael Thornburg, Charles Barnes, and Burnis Barrett. They are *friends*.

Perhaps renewal in our time is too much to expect. We have been a long time at the process of winding and wrapping, tying ourselves both up and down with the fetters of yesterday. There are only two ways out: to unwind ourselves or for Christ to "break the chains which fetter you and me." My *prayer* is the latter, of course. But my *determination* is to start on the former. Perhaps we shall not see the Church liberated from itself in our lifetime, but *let us begin.* Elton Trueblood once said:

> A man has made at least a start on discovering the meaning of human life when he plants shade trees under which he knows full well he will never sit.

Here, then, is my seedling.

DAVID P. HANEY

Pastor's Study
Annapolis, Maryland

THE CHURCH, O LORD, IS THINE

MARION

David P. Haney   *Arthur H. Messiter*

1. The Church, O Lord, is Thine, Is Thine for - ev - er more;
2. The Church, O Lord, is theirs, Whose toil this day hath brought;
3. The Church, O Lord, is ours, Is ours at high - est cost:
4. The Church, O Lord, is mine, And to its call I yield;
5. The Church, O Lord, is Thine, And we who bear Thy name,

From age to age, from pole to pole, And from both shore to shore.
Their faith, their hope and fearless love, Our her - i - tage hath bought.
Thy Cross, its shame and sac - ri - fice And all the mar - tyred host.
To be as scat - tered, liv - ing seed In God's own har - vest field.
Un - til that Day Thou bearest it away, Fault-less and with-out blame.

REFRAIN

Thy Church,   Thy Church,   Thy Church for - ev - er more.
Thy Church,   Thy Church,

PART ONE

Chapter One

Bible Study Selection

'The kingdom of Heaven is like treasure lying buried in a field. The man who found it, buried it again; and for sheer joy went and *sold everything he had,* and bought that field.

'Here is another picture of the kingdom of Heaven. A merchant looking out for fine pearls found one of very special value; so he went and *sold everything he had,* and bought it.

'Again the kingdom of Heaven is like a net let down into the sea, where fish of every kind were caught in it. When it was full, it was dragged ashore. Then the men sat down and collected the good fish into pails and threw the worthless away. That is how it will be at the end of time. The angels will go forth, and they will separate the wicked from the good, and throw them into the blazing furnace, the place of wailing and grinding of teeth.

'Have you understood all this?' he asked; and they answered, 'Yes.' He said to them, 'When, therefore, a teacher of the law has become a learner in the kingdom of Heaven, he is like a householder who can produce from his store both the new and the old.'

(Matt. 13:44-52 NEB, italics added)

THE KINGDOM

"Here and Now" or "There and Then"?

> *We are a huge way off from
> the kingdom of God.*
>
> JEREMY TAYLOR

All paths of inquiry concerning the present and the future of Christianity and the Gospel must ultimately arrive at the question of the Church, its nature and function. For many today a very good question is, "What shall we do with the Church?" The better question, however, is: "What is the Church to do?" This properly focuses the question on the *purpose* of the Church. But that purpose is not ours to decide — it is Christ's. This forces us, then, to raise the *right* question: How did Christ envision the Church? or, How does it fit into His strategy?

Those committed to Christ's Church and to its renewal in our time are also committed to a basic premise: that renewal will come only as we successfully activate the laity. The activation and deployment of the vast lay forces is priority business for the Church today simply because they are intrinsic to authentic Christianity. Biblically the laity, the *laos* (the "People of God"), are the "ministers" of Christ. Not "pastors," mind you, but "ministers"; for the pastor's ministry is to equip the ministers (Eph. 4:11, 12). This, *The Idea of the Laity*, is a basic assumption to both the New Testament and renewal. Most of the Church, however, operates on other assumptions — most of them unexamined and many of them invalid. It is for this reason that we must collectively pause at this point on the Church's journey and examine purposes. And the place to begin is not in enunciating a "theology of the laity," but rather with the question, "What is God up to in the world, and how does the Church fit into it?" Beyond all our techniques, methods, mechanics, organization, and structures, we will see our proper role only from the perspective of *God's* intentions. Having grasped that, we can then move beyond our assumptions to proper activity in and with the Church.

The often unseen truth, however, is that Christ said very little about the Church! There are but two references to Christ's use of the word "church":

> And I tell you, you are Peter, and on this rock I will build my church, and the powers of death shall not prevail against it.   (Matt. 16:18)[1]

> If your brother sins against you, go and tell him his fault, between you and him alone. If he listens to you, you have gained your brother. But if he does not listen, take one or two others along with you, that every word may be confirmed by the evidence of two or three witnesses. If he refuses to listen to them, tell it to the church; and if he refuses to listen even to the church, let him be to you as a Gentile and a tax collector.
>
> (Matt. 18:15-17)

And that's it. This is true because "church" was simply not His word for the God Movement. Nor was it "Christianity." His expression was "the kingdom of God." [2]

---

[1] All Scripture quotations are from *The Revised Standard Version* unless otherwise noted.

[2] "Kingdom of God" and "kingdom of Heaven" are being treated as synonyms by the author. See *The Interpreter's Dictionary of the Bible*, Vol. 3. (Nashville: Abingdon, 1962), pp. 17-18.

THE WHAT OF THE KINGDOM.   Many of our present problems with Christian strategy are the result of our failure to see the kingdom of God as prior to the Church. Yet only a cursory examination of the gospels is necessary to see its preeminence in the mind of Christ.

When John the Baptist began his introductory ministry for the Christ, it was with the words: "the *kingdom* . . . is at hand" (Matt. 3:1, 2; italics added for emphasis throughout chapter). When Jesus launched His public ministry, the gospel writer is careful to say, He "came preaching and bringing the good news of the *kingdom*" (Luke 8:1). The first request He taught us to make in prayer was "Thy *kingdom* come" (Matt. 6:10). His great message, the Sermon on the Mount, begins with the Beatitude, "Blessed are the poor in spirit, for theirs is the *kingdom* . . ." (Matt. 5:3), and it reaches its climax with the central truth: "Seek ye first the *kingdom*" (Matt. 6:33). Indeed, most of Christ's preaching was in parables, and most of His parables begin, "The *kingdom* is like unto . . ."

The new birth, Jesus said, is necessary because without it no one can see or enter "the *kingdom*" (John 3:1-7). Those who follow Him are not to "look back" for such are "unfit for the *kingdom*" (Luke 9:62).

When Christ faced temptation in the wilderness, the central temptation had to do with the *kingdoms* of the world (Luke 4:5-7). When He sent the disciples on their first preaching mission, His orders were "to preach the *kingdom* of God" (Luke 9:2). Indeed, the whole missionary enterprise has its focus in the kingdom!

> And this gospel of the kingdom will be preached throughout the whole world, as a testimony to all nations; and then the end will come.   (Matt. 24:14)

Christ spoke of His second coming as seeing "the Son of man coming in His *kingdom*" (Matt. 16:28). As they prepared for His death in the Upper Room, He took the cup and said He would drink of it no more until "I drink it new with you in my Father's *kingdom*" (Matt. 26:29).

At His trial Jesus said very little, as Isaiah had predicted (53:7), but when He spoke it was about His *kingdom* not being "of this world" (John 18:36).

On the cross He took time to speak to a penitent thief about being with Him that day in the *kingdom* (Luke 23: 42, 43). It is extremely significant that, during His forty days of post-resurrection companying with the disciples, He spoke of "the *kingdom* of God" (Acts 1:3). And even at the last moment before the Ascension, the conversation still had to do with the *kingdom* (Acts 1:6).

Do you see it? The *kingdom* was His magnificent obsession! The *kingdom,* not the *Church!* What then is it? The kingdom of God represents what God is up to in this world! And it represents the "clue" for which we seek as we seek renewal, for the kingdom is the unifying theme of the Bible from the ancient prophets to the Book of Revelation.

> The wolf shall dwell with the lamb, and the leopard shall lie down with the kid, and the calf and the lion and the fatling together, and a little child shall lead them. The cow and the bear shall feed; their young shall lie down together; and the lion shall eat straw like the ox. The sucking child shall play over the hole of the asp, and the weaned child shall put his hand on the adder's den. They shall not hurt or destroy in all my holy mountain; for the earth shall be full of the knowledge of the LORD as the waters cover the sea.
>
> (Isa. 11:6-9)

> Then the seventh angel blew his trumpet, and there were loud voices in heaven, saying, "The kingdom of the world has become the kingdom of our Lord and of his Christ, and he shall reign for ever and ever."
>
> (Rev. 11:15)

The kingdom is the time when we will beat our swords into plowshares and our spears into pruning hooks, when nation will not lift up sword against nation, and we will study war no more (Mic. 4:3). It is the era of ultimate, consummate brotherhood and peace; when the *kingdoms* of the world become the kingdom of God, and no one will have to teach another of the Lord for all will know Him (Jer. 31:34). It will be no less than a "new humanity" (Eph. 2:15 NEB) in which there is neither Jew nor Greek, bond nor free, male nor female (Gal. 3:28).

THE WHEN AND WHERE OF THE KINGDOM. But "when" and "where" is the kingdom? We are left with the paradox that "it *is*, yet is *to be*." As presented in the Bible, the kingdom is at once *coming, at hand,* and *existingly present.* The kingdom is not a particular nation; rather "many will come from east and west and sit . . . in the kingdom" (Matt. 8:11). It is not a worldly kingdom, as Jesus said to Pilate (John 18:36), yet it is "in the midst" of the world (Luke 17:21). It has a corporate nature to be sure, but it is intensely personal: it is "within you." [3]

When and where, then? Suffice it to say that the kingdom of God *is* . . . whenever and wherever God is King! Thus, to whatever extent — whenever or wherever — God is in control, the kingdom has come. It could be a person, a group, a congregation, a nation; but wherever God is King — there is the kingdom of God. As Carl F. H. Henry says: "The Kingdom of God is *now* for everyone who receives Him as Savior and Lord." [4]

In a very real sense, whenever men work for peace and brotherhood, wherever sickness and disease and poverty are fought, whenever injustice is corrected and the abused are protected, it is evidence that men long for that kingdom to come: whatever they may call it, be their definition Christian or not. The heart of man and the heart of God evidence their unity at this point. Whether it is a physician treating malnutrition, a lawyer fighting discrimination, a politician seeking better housing or waging

[3] See the RSV marginal note. Luke 17:21.
[4] Carl F. H. Henry. *The God Who Shows Himself.* (Waco: Word, 1966), p. 100.

peace: the goal is the same as God's. This is what God wants too! But the clue which the Christian carries gives him the immeasurable advantage in its accomplishment: he not only shares the *goal*, he knows the *means*, too! He knows that the kingdom can never be realized without the King!

THE WORTH OF THE KINGDOM. It was this kingdom which Jesus saw as worth more than all. His call to us to "seek first his kingdom" (Matt. 6:33) indicates He viewed it as the most valuable thing on earth. It was this kingdom alone which merited His life . . . and death.

Nowhere did He more clearly portray the ultimate worthiness of the Kingdom than with two parables in Matthew 13:

> The kingdom of heaven is like treasure hidden in a field, which a man found and covered up; then in his joy he goes and *sells all* that he has and buys that field.

> Again, the kingdom of heaven is like a merchant in search of fine pearls, who, on finding one pearl of great value, went and *sold all* that he had and bought it.
>
> (Matt. 13:44-46, italics added)

It is this "worth-all-ness" of the kingdom which must capture and captivate the Church today, just as it did Christ. It must rank first — *before all* other claims upon our lives. *The kingdom!* It is here, at the point of the kingdom, that we meet the heart and the plan of God and find our clue. This kingdom is what He is up to in our world and, consequently, what the "children of the kingdom" are to be about, also. It is the vision without which we perish for want of a purpose.

With the recognition of the clue, however, also comes the recognition that we are yet a huge way off from the kingdom of God. But lift up your hearts:

> "It is your Father's good pleasure to give you the kingdom."
>
> (Luke 12:32)

DISCUSSION QUESTIONS

Discussion questions are included for each chapter to provide a springboard for group discussion. The group must keep in mind that the *purpose* of discussion in renewal groups is *practical,* not theoretical. "Good discussion" is not a "good argument"; rather, it is that which helps and encourages and strengthens. It would be wise for the group to read Chapter Four and Appendix A prior to the first discussion period. A "Creative Group Procedure" is given to use in addition to, or in place of, the discussion. Approximately 30 minutes should be allotted if the procedures are used; one hour if both the questions and procedures are used.

1. Let the group discussion "emerge" around the central idea of the chapter, that God is not *first* gathering a Church, but establishing a kingdom and that the Church exists to bring it to pass.

2. Using the prophetic passages mentioned in the chapter, and any others, discuss what the world would be like were the kingdom actualized today.

3. Discuss how the group will begin to accept the "worth-all-illness" of the kingdom and what effects can be anticipated.

CREATIVE GROUP PROCEDURE

In an effort to "open up" the groups at the first meeting, *start* the sessions (before the study) with the "Quaker Questions" (see p. 61). If these have been used previously, use the following questions, asking them one at a time, allowing the entire group to answer each question before proceeding to the next question. (1) My favorite time of the year is; (2) My favorite place in the house is; (3) My favorite part of the worship service is; (4) If God were to withdraw from the world entirely, the thing I would miss most about Him is.

Chapter Two

Bible Study Selection

You Gentiles by birth — who are called the uncircumcised by the Jews, who call themselves the circumcised (which refers to what men themselves do on their bodies) — remember what you were in the past. At that time you were apart from Christos. You were foreigners, and did not belong to God's own chosen people. You had no part in the covenants, which were based on God's promises to his people. You lived in this world without hope and without God. But now, in union with Christ Jesus, you who used to be far away have been brought near by the death of Christ. For Christ himself has brought us peace, by making the *Jews and Gentiles one people*. With his own body he broke down the wall that separated them and kept them enemies. He abolished the Jewish Law, with its commandments and rules, in order to create out of the two races one new people in union with himself, in this way making peace. By his death on the cross Christ destroyed the enmity; by means of the cross he united both races into one body and brought them back to God. So Christ came and preached the Good News of peace *to all* — to you Gentiles, who were far away from God, and to the Jews, who were near to Him. It is through Christ that all of us, Jews and Gentiles, are able to come in the one Spirit into the presence of the Father.

So then, you Gentiles are not foreigners or strangers any longer; you are now *fellow-citizens* with God's people, and members of the family of God. You, too, are built upon the foundation laid by the apostles and prophets, the cornerstone being Christ Jesus himself. He is the one who holds the whole building together and makes it grow into a sacred temple in the Lord. In union with him you too are being built together with all the others into a house where God lives through his Spirit.

(Eph. 2:11-22 TEV, italics added)

THE CHURCH

To Serve or to Survive?

> *The Kingdom of God is mirrored in the fellowship of the redeemed who seek to do God's will on earth.*
> Carl F. H. Henry

If the kingdom is prior to the Church, where does the *Church* fit into the strategy of God? The question of just what the Church is to be and to do is perhaps the most pressing question facing us today. That it is called to do something is shown by the word we translate as "church": *ekklesia.* It is from the root verb *kaleo* meaning "to call." The Church has a "calling," but what is it?

It is my contention that the mission of the Church is fully seen only from the perspective of the kingdom of God. The kingdom is the *goal* and the Church exists as the *agent* to bring it to pass. Thus, we may say that the Church is the *local branch office* of the kingdom. It is the visible "outcropping" of the invisible kingdom, as P. T. Forsyth called it. It is the *verifying laboratory specimen* of the fact that the kingdom of God is a working possibility rather than a subjective ideal.

As the working agency of the kingdom, the local church

exists for a two-fold purpose: (1) to demonstrate the king-dom and (2) to spread it. As W. O. Carver put it:

> The church is the core of God's kingdom as being real-ized in human history. Local churches are the agencies of that kingdom and of its gospel; thus they are 'colo-nies' of the kingdom of heaven on earth, located in the midst of the world which is to be won through the gospel. They are not only emigration centers for heaven but are also recruiting agencies and training instru-ments and supervising bodies for the recruits as they become active workers in the gospel. [1]

DEMONSTRATING THE KINGDOM. As a Spirit-gathered col-lection of surrendered spirits, the local church is to be on permanent display, exhibiting the workability of the king-dom *idea:* that "in Christ" there is no division, no partiality. The kingdom promises that all the dividing walls may be torn down; that Jew and Greek, bond and free may be-come *one*.

> For he is himself our peace. Gentiles and Jews, he has made the two one, and in his own body of flesh and blood has broken down the enmity which stood like a dividing wall between them; for he annulled the law with its rules and regulations, so as to create out of the two a single new humanity in himself, thereby making peace. This was his purpose, to reconcile the two in a single body to God through the cross, on which he killed the enmity. So he came and proclaimed the good news: peace to you who were far off, and peace to those who were near by; for through him we both alike have access to the Father in the one Spirit. Thus you are no longer aliens in a foreign land, but fellow-citizens with God's people, members of God's household.
>
> (Eph. 2:14-19 NEB)

Thus the continuing daily life in the churches is to be irrefutable evidence that *community* is a working option . . . in Christ. Colin Williams says it is to manifest "that

[1] W. O. Carver. *What Is the Church?* (Nashville: Broadman, 1958), p. 13.

it is possible for conflicts of race, culture, class and sex"
to be overcome and that a fellowship can "emerge beyond
these ancient hostilities." [2] Thus, to a dividing and splin-
tered world, the *churches* constitute the city set on a hill,
showing the Way to the kingdom.

The best illustration of it, simply because it was intended
as a foreshadowing of the kingdom, was the gathering together of the nation of Israel. It is a common misconcep-
tion that the Israelites in bondage in Egypt were a unified
nation, but they were not. At best, they were but an amal-
gamation of scattered, warring, hostile Bedouin tribes which
had been captured one by one over a period of many years.
They were Semites, to be sure, but with little in common —
so were the Canaanites, Perizzites, and Amalekites. They
were the *habiru* (from which we get the word "Hebrew"),
meaning that they were wandering peoples without political
ties. They were literally people without citizenship who
collected and scattered into the desert regions to war and
to pilfer.

They were "not a people" whom God made *one;* they
became "His people"! And God's choice was deliberate.
There is more to Ogden Nash's couplet than meets the eye:

> How odd
> Of God
> To choose
> The Jews.

God took these disconnected groups, formerly hostile
to others and even among themselves, and welded them
together with but one common bond: their God! Hosea
relearned it vividly when God instructed him to sym-
bolically name his third child *Lo-ammi:* "Not my people."
But notice the full context.

> Then said God, Call his name Lo-ammi: for ye are not
> my people, and I will not be your God. Yet the number
> of the children of Israel shall be as the sand of the sea,

[2] Colin Williams. *New Directions In Theology Today,* Vol. 4, *The
Church.* (Philadelphia: Westminster, 1968), p. 90.

which cannot be measured nor numbered; and it shall come to pass, that in the place where it was said unto them, Ye are not my people. there it shall be said unto them, Ye are the sons of the living God.

(Hos. 1:9, 10 KJV)

They were "not a people." But they became "a people"; God made them *His* people.

This was the same pattern Jesus followed as He began to gather His new people together. Nowhere is it more clearly seen than in including both Levi and Simon the Zealot in the apostolic band. Levi was a publican, one who had sold out to Rome, a traitor to Israel. Simon, on the other hand, was a Zealot, a revolutionary. His creed was simple: no king but Yahweh, no law but Moses, no tax but the Temple tax. Never could two men be more incompatible and hostile. Clarence Jordan surmises that more than one night Jesus had to sleep between them! Indeed, Jordan says, "The only thing that kept Simon's knife out of Matthew's ribs was Jesus."[3] But it said to the world that a demonstration was under way — a demonstration of the kingdom. It is no wonder that Peter chose Hosea's theme to express it.

> But ye are a chosen generation, a royal priesthood, an holy nation, a peculiar people; that ye should shew forth the praises of him who hath called you out of darkness into his marvellous light: Which in time past were not a people, but are now the people of God.
>
> (1 Peter 2:9, 10 KJV)

Then God chose to widen the circle by including the Gentiles, also! Paul called it the "mystery hidden for the ages" but now revealed that *through the Church* the complete purposes of God are being made manifest (Eph. 2: 11 - 3:13; 5:21-33; Col. 1:24-27).

The New Testament word for the fulfillment of this task of demonstrating the kingdom is *koinonia*. It is the Greek

---

[3] Dallas Lee, ed. *The Substance of Faith and Other Cotton Patch Sermons by Clarence Jordan.* (New York: Association Press, 1972), p. 61.

word for "fellowship," but it means far more than after-service Cokes and coffee, Sunday school class socials, and slogans like "The End of Your Search for a Friendly Church." Bound up in its definition is an unbreakable bond of love, an inexhaustible reservoir of concern, a fail-safe unity.

Our record, however, indicates that much is to be desired with our demonstrating ability: we have not yet achieved it! John H. Paterson rightly calls it "the missing evidence." [4] We have yet to reverse the trend which began with Cain and Abel! Church splits and squabbles are common fare in the current criticism (and rejection) of the Church as an alternative to the world's way. We have yet to bridge the gap between internal disagreement and disunity. The most indicting element, however, is the *pettiness* of most of it! Somehow we have failed to see that love is neither an ideal nor a suggestion; it is a *command* (John 15:12).

Called to *demonstrate* the kingdom, we most often *negate* it by what we are and the way we act.

To be sure, division existed in the apostolic era, and we have always had to "guard the unity." One reason for our failure at it, however, is that we have frequently posted the wrong guards. We have sought to force and/or enforce unity by commonly accepted creeds, rituals, requirements, and organization. These have their necessary purposes, but unity is not one of them. The unity of which the Bible speaks is *of the Spirit*. Unity is a by-product of the act of yielding to the Spirit's control and leadership in our personal relationships within the community of faith. The "fruits of the Spirit," those things most necessary to unity (love, joy, peace, patience, kindness, goodness, faithfulness, gentleness, self-control) are to be found no other place: they are *His* fruit (Gal. 5:22). Thus, while Paul urged unity, he made it clear that it was "the unity of the Spirit" (Eph. 4:3).

And this fact yet stands: we are called to *demonstrate* the kingdom in the churches and before the world; anything

[4] John H. Paterson. *The Greatness of Christ.* (New Jersey: Revell, 1962), p. 43.

less is sin, especially in our present global village where there is no longer any place to hide from one another. What has always been our spiritual mission is now a physical mandate for both the Church and civilization.

SPREADING THE KINGDOM.   Merely to demonstrate the kingdom of God, however, is to fall short of our full calling. In a sense, this would result in Amish-like clusters whose demonstration of the kingdom may be admired, but whose influence is more protected than propagated. The Church is called not only to demonstrate the kingdom but also to spread it. This has been essential to the God Movement from the beginning. Christ did not organize a band of hermit monks; He called His early band "apostles" — from the verb meaning "to send forth." His style of training involved sending them out on missions "to preach the kingdom of God" (Luke 9:2). As Elton Trueblood has pointed out, all the metaphors Christ used indicate the task of penetrating the world: salt, light, keys, bread, water, leaven and fire.

> At first the variety of these figures is bewildering, but a powerful insight comes when we realize, suddenly, what they have in common. Each figure represents some kind of penetration. The purpose of the salt is to penetrate the meat and thus preserve it; the function of light is to penetrate the darkness; the only use of the keys is to penetrate the lock; bread is worthless until it penetrates the body; water penetrates the hard crust of earth; leaven penetrates the dough, to make it rise; fire continues only as it reaches new fuel, and the best way to extinguish it is to contain it.

> The cumulative effect of all these figures is almost overwhelming. In any case, they make absolutely clear what the function of Christ's company is meant to be. [5]

Indeed, Christ's last recorded words were words of commission.

[5] Elton Trueblood. *Company of the Committed.* (New York: Harper & Row, 1961), pp. 68-69.

> Go therefore and make disciples of all nations, baptiz-
> ing them in the name of the Father and of the Son and
> of the Holy Spirit, teaching them to observe all that I
> have commanded you; and lo, I am with you always,
> to the close of the age. (Matt. 28:19, 20)

And in the Acts:

> But you shall receive power when the Holy Spirit has
> come upon you; and you shall be my witnesses in Jeru-
> salem and in all Judea and Samaria and to the end of
> the earth. (Acts 1:8)

No question about it — we are to spread the kingdom!
But *how?* There is no more divisive topic among Chris-
tians today than the methods of evangelism. It is true that
Paul said "by all means" (1 Cor. 9:22), but the rest of the
New Testament qualifies his use of "all."

We have tried coercion and legislation as a means to the
kingdom, with little success and much failure. Peter sought
to preserve the kingdom's King with the sword (Luke 22:
38, 47-51) and Constantine, Calvin, and the Puritans were
all in his futile train. The manner of spreading the kingdom
which Jesus had in mind had to do with proclamation: an-
nouncing its possibility and encouraging its acceptance —
but not *forcing* it. Both Calvinists and Arminians, and any
combination thereof, must acknowledge the element of vol-
untary choice in accepting the good news of the kingdom's
possibility in a person's life. Christ did. He never violated
it. And we must never forget it.

We spread the kingdom by witness, by proclamation: that
the good news *is the kingdom* (note how the expression is
repeatedly made "the good news *of the kingdom*") and that
the way to the kingdom is by way of God's appointed King.
Among the Church's "forgottens" and "overlookeds" today
is also the emphatic element that Christ-the-King is *alone*
the Way to the kingdom. People may accept our ideas, our
"plans," our organizations, even our creeds, but if they do
not accept our Christ, they go away empty-hearted.

The demonstration and the spreading of the kingdom by

the Church are inextricably bound together. They are halves of a whole. When one is deficient, so is the other; when one is missing, the other is inconsequential. And the truth is: we are now failing at *both*.

Part of our present failure to demonstrate and to spread the kingdom of God is due to the panic over the Church's ability to survive, let alone serve. As our statistics continue to decline from the highs of the 1950s, we have focused all our existing energies on . . . *existing!* But the Church, in its high times and its lows, always and ever exists to function, not merely to exist. Indeed, we live and live on only as we die! One of the most poignant symbols in our Heritage Baptist Church building in Annapolis is found in the lower corner of a beautiful stained glass Resurrection window: *the bursting pomegranate.* [6] It is an early and seldom-remembered symbol of the Faith: as the pomegranate dies, it bursts asunder . . . *spreading the seeds of its own continued life!* D. T. Niles was right on target when he said:

> The world doesn't owe the Church a living; the Church owes the world its own true life . . . [7]

The Church exists to demonstrate the kingdom of God and then to spread it. It is no less than our call from Christ and our debt to the world.

Discussion Questions

1. Remembering that the group exists to help sharpen one another's swords, not to use them on each other, discuss the practical ways of beginning to *demonstrate the kingdom* within your group.

2. What difference should it make within the group to accept the verb "to love" as a *command* rather than a suggestion or an ideal? (John 15:12)

[6] The sanctuary of the Heritage Baptist Church of Annapolis has four lovely stained glass windows depicting the Incarnation, the Crucifixion, the Resurrection, and Pentecost.

[7] Quoted in: Williams. *Op. cit.*, pp. 16-17.

3. In what specific ways can the groups, collectively and separately, begin to *spread* the kingdom?

CREATIVE GROUP PROCEDURE

Let the group write a "group covenant" centering on the idea of demonstrating and spreading the kingdom. This will not be an "I believe" document so much as a "This I will do" covenant with each other. It should begin with "We covenant together as a group and as individuals who seek to take Christ seriously to. . . ." Perhaps the group could divide into two groups, one working on the "demonstrating" section, the other on the "spreading" aspect. The group may want to officially adopt the covenant.

Chapter Three

Bible Study Selection

Now those who were scattered because of the persecution that arose over Stephen traveled as far as Phoenicia and Cyprus and Antioch, speaking the word to none except Jews. But there were some of them, men of Cyprus and Cyrene, who on coming to Antioch spoke to the Greeks also, preaching the Lord Jesus. And the hand of the Lord was with them, and a great number that believed turned to the Lord. News of this came to the ears of the church in Jerusalem, and they sent Barnabas to Antioch. When he came and saw the grace of God, he was glad; and he exhorted them all to remain faithful to the Lord with steadfast purpose; for he was a good man, full of the Holy Spirit and of faith. And a large company was added to the Lord. So Barnabas went to Tarsus *to look for Saul;* and when he had found him, he brought him to Antioch. For a whole year they met with the church, and taught a large company of people; and in Antioch the disciples were for the first time called Christians.

(Acts 11:19-26 RSV, italics added)

CHAPTER THREE

THE MINISTRY

Torchbearer or Lamplighter?

> *You must teach others the things which you and many witnesses have heard me speak about. Teach these great truths to trustworthy men who will, in turn, pass them on to others.*
>
> PAUL TO TIMOTHY

One no sooner accepts the challenge of the Church to demonstrate and spread the kingdom of God than he runs head-on into the problem of the ministry. How the Church is to implement its call inevitably has to do with the ministry: *who is to do it?*

"Ministry" is that catchall which gathers up all the working responsibilities of the churches, but its current definition is fuzzy at best. "Identity crisis" is an overworked label in our culture, but it does help to isolate the source of the present clergy-laity-ministry impasse: *ambiguity.* "What's a preacher to do?" "What are laymen for?" Given the priority of the kingdom of God, and the function of the Church as the local branch office to demonstrate and spread it, where does the *pastor* fit in? The current answer is: the pastor is to do the Church's work, or at least he is doing it even if he is not supposed to do it — a sort of *ministry by default.*

39

FROM A VERB TO A NOUN. Somewhere between A.D. 33 and the present, "minister" moved both grammatically and theologically from a verb (a thing done) to a noun (a person doing it); what was originally a *function of* the Church became a *station in* the Church. That is, "ministry" was originally the assignment of all believers; indeed, each follower had his own ministry or ministries. These were gifts and callings of the Spirit. The pastor existed as the one whose gift and call it was to equip the ministers (laity) for their ministries. Paul's letter to the congregation at Ephesus is the best available presentation of this concept which Luther was later to label "the priesthood of [all] the believers."

> I entreat you, then — I, a prisoner for the Lord's sake: as God has called you, live up to your calling. . . . *But each of us has been given his gift,* his due portion of Christ's bounty. Therefore Scripture says:
>
> > He ascended into the heights
> > With captives in his train;
> > He gave gifts to men. . . .
>
> And these were his gifts: some to be apostles, some prophets, some evangelists, some pastors and teachers, *to equip God's people* for work in his service, to the building up of the body of Christ. So shall we all at last attain to the unity inherent in our faith and our knowledge of the Son of God — to mature manhood, measured by nothing less than the full stature of Christ. We are no longer to be children, tossed by the waves and whirled about by every fresh gust of teaching, dupes of crafty rogues and their deceitful schemes. No, let us speak the truth in love; so shall we fully grow up into Christ. He is the head, and on him the whole body depends. Bonded and knit together by every constituent joint, the whole frame grows *through the due activity of each part,* and builds itself up in love.
>
> (Eph. 4:1, 7, 8, 11-16 NEB, italics added)

Paul emphasizes that each one has his own call and that some are called to be pastors and teachers *to equip* the people for *their ministries.* The pastor's ministry is to equip the ministers (laity), not to do the work for them!

When Paul passed through Ephesus for what he thought was the last time, he called together the elders (a term including both pastors and lay leaders) of the church at Ephesus and charged them with the responsibilities which are now solely (and wrongly) considered the pastor's alone.

> Take heed to yourselves and to all the flock, in which the Holy Spirit has made you overseers, to care for the church of God which he obtained with the blood of his own Son.   (Acts 20:28)

This same pattern is repeatedly evidenced among the New Testament churches. Paul left Titus on the island of Crete to "appoint elders" who were able to "give instruction" (Titus 1:5-9). And among Paul's last instructions to Timothy was this:

> So, my son, be strong in the grace that Christ Jesus gives. Everything that you have heard me teach in public you should in turn entrust to reliable men, who will be able to pass it on to others.
>   (2 Tim. 2:1, 2 *Phillips*)

But somewhere, somehow, "ministry" became a noun; the absence of the biblical emphasis led not only to the restriction of ministry to the professional clergy, but to additional assignments neither his nor the New Testament's. Indeed, the present-day pastor's *priority* list is anything but his *assignment* list! Most of what he is required (or expected) to do is drawn from a model established in the rural culture of the century just passed, a model designed for an age whose schedule was built around farming seasons and the speed of horses. One recent seminary graduate said to me: "I was programed for a passing age!"

The present "pro" is looked upon by pulpit committees (notice the singling out of one function, an irony in light of what they expect in addition to his pulpit duties) as a man with a panacea for their parish problems. The unspoken but statistically verifiable evidence is that they will give him two and one-half years to accomplish it. He has a program and they agree to underwrite it. He is the man with the answers. (Quite candidly, some of us pastors cultivate this "answer-man" image with an attitude akin to the man's who said of his mother-in-law: "She may not always be right, but she's never wrong!") He is to visit, counsel, preach, teach, administer, build buildings, raise funds, prepare bulletins and newsletters, marry, bury, motivate, and be active in civic affairs, the local ministerium, and the denomination.

Indeed, the "perfect pastor" has been described as one who preaches exactly twenty minutes and then sits down. He condemns sin, but never hurts anyone's feelings. He labors from 8:00 A.M. to 10:00 P.M. in every kind of work, from preaching to custodial service. He makes $60 a week, wears good clothes, buys good books regularly, has a nice family, drives a good car, and gives $30 a week to the church. He also stands ready to contribute to every good work that comes along. The ideal pastor is twenty-six years old and has been preaching for thirty years. He is at once tall and short, thin and heavy-set, and handsome. He has one brown eye and one blue; his hair is parted in the middle with left side dark and straight and the right side brown and wavy. He has a burning desire to work with teenagers and spends all his time with the older folks. He smiles all the time with a straight face because he has a sense of humor that keeps him seriously dedicated to his work. He makes fifteen calls a day on church members, spends all his time evangelizing the unchurched, and is never out of his office!

One could add a similar list of expectations for his family, especially his wife. One 200-member congregation of my knowledge found itself one Sunday with its pastor ill; his wife, after calling and being refused by all the male leadership, had to deliver the morning sermon in a denomination which would sooner die than ordain women! Moreover, any pastor knows his stock is higher if his wife plays the organ or piano.

Of course, this kind of expectation means the pastor is not on tenure, but on the merit system. If his preaching, programing, promoting, and personality do not produce the promised panacea — "they" know what to do! Within a one-week period recently, I counseled a young pastor one year out of seminary who was leaving the ministry a broken man; put his wife in contact with a psychiatrist; received a call from one pastor and a letter from another — both classmates of mine and both seeking secular employment. "They" are running us off — and "we" are leaving — at the rate of 10,000 a year in the United States! Called to do one thing and forced to do another, burdened with unauthorized assignments and wearied by the schedule, we are now face-to-face with the truth that, as Thomes Mullen said, we have the men fit for the ministry, but not a ministry fit for the men! The Church has its *victors*, to be sure, but it also has its *victims*.

Yet the accompanying truth, which must be said in behalf of clergy and laity alike, is that neither group intends or wants this situation. Where, then, shall we turn? *Why not to the New Testament?*

FROM TORCHBEARER TO LAMPLIGHTER. The New Testament pattern of ministry is that the pastor is not the *torchbearer*, the one out in the front leading the way ("Stick close to me"), but the *lighter of lamps*. As Elton Trueblood expressed it: the current idea is that the pastor is one who has a program, and the people exist to support his ministry; the New Testament idea is that the people have a program, and the pastor exists to support them. [1] Nowhere was this better expressed than on an outdoor church bulletin board in New York City; just below the schedule of services it read:

Ministers: All of the Members
Assistant to the Ministers: The Pastor

There is the answer! A return to the *original* strategy! Moreover, it is not only scriptural but logical: just the sheer

[1] Elton Trueblood. *The Incendiary Fellowship.* (New York: Harper & Row, 1965), p. 53.

numbers involved force the conclusion that the task of ministry (demonstrating and spreading the kingdom) is too much for any minority, no matter how gifted or trained they may be. [2] The schedule is simply too much and people in need are too many for a pastor-only approach. The New Testament strategy is that the Church — the laity and clergy *together* — constitutes "a royal priesthood" (1 Peter 2:9); indeed, an entire "kingdom of priests" (Rev. 5:10). Ministry is a *function* for all, not a *station* for a few. The pastor is not the *torchbearer;* he is the *lamplighter.*

Richard Niebuhr views this *functional* concept as both a reversion to the New Testament and "the new pattern" for today. The Pastor is no longer to operate primarily from the pulpit, but from his study. Niebuhr likens this to a return "to the ancient bishop, whose task was not so much to oversee a far-flung diocese as to *edify* the local congregation." [3]

Will it work? The answer to that, of course, is another question: *if it is New Testament, why ask?* Do it! [4] But how?

The first step toward the renewal of the Church in our time is to clarify the concept of "ministry." Perhaps our difficult task is to break through the encrusted definition of what is presently meant by "minister." Biblically it means that *every follower* of Christ has a specific calling (or callings); that *every believer* has a gift (or gifts) which brings a unique contribution to the local body of believers and is to be employed in the total kingdom enterprise. We have limited this concept to the professional clergy, "the called"; but wrongly so. It is said that Michelangelo once entered the studio of his student Raphael and, upon view-

[2] Trueblood. *Company of the Committed,* p. 60.

[3] From *The Future Shape of Ministry* by Urban T. Holmes, III. Copyright © 1971 by The Seabury Press, Inc. Used by permission.

[4] This is not to say it has not been done. The reader is urged to read such reports as Elizabeth O'Connor's *Call to Commitment* (New York: Harper & Row, 1968); Ralph Neighbour's *The Seven Last Words of the Church* (Grand Rapids: Zondervan, 1973); Robert C. Girard's *Brethren, Hang Loose* (Grand Rapids: Zondervan, 1972).

ing one of his landscapes, took a piece of chalk and wrote across it, "Amplius!" *Larger!* Raphael's perspective was too small. Our concept of ministry must also be amplified — it is too small! *All* believers are included in the New Testament definition of ministry. But, if this is the case, what is the *pastor* supposed to do? First, he is to be . . .

The Preparer of His People. His primary function is to equip his people for their ministries. This is not to say he is exempted from ministry; he is a "playing coach," as Samuel Shoemaker stated it, or the "working foreman." But he must firmly resolve to stop doing ministry *for* the people and to start doing it *to* them.

This resolve will have its own set of implications. As one can readily see mirrored in the equipping ministry of Christ, he must leave the crowds for the clusters — the Sunday morning congregations for the small groups. Likewise, he will begin to look at his church program to see if it is geared to equip . . . or to entertain. Then the needed changes will begin to emerge.

Mostly, however, he will begin to look for the "ministries" bound up in the followers, and for ways of releasing them. The crowds saw in Levi, the tax collector, only the empty and dirtied soul of one who had sold out his nation. But Jesus saw a "Matthew" inside Levi! He saw a "rock" in Simon and "fishers of men" in James and John. Thus the pastor begins to see people more in terms of their potential than their actual. He will begin to "cull out the called-out," looking for multipliers, for the potentially powerful. And having found the-person-Christ-would-make and the-gift-He-has-given, the pastor will exercise his own ministry by polishing and preparing the minister for ministry. The discoverer becomes the enabler and, hence, a lighter of lamps. That is authentic New Testament pastoral ministry!

It is like Barnabas discovering and uncovering the ministry of Paul in Antioch. Years before, Barnabas had filed away Paul's statement of his call to the Gentiles. It was an idea too radical to handle then. But when Barnabas visited the Antioch congregation as an emissary from the Jerusalem church and saw the Gentile phenomenon coming to pass, he remembered and went to Tarsus to get Paul! He matched *man* with *ministry* — in effect "creating" Paul! (Acts 11: 19-26) It is like Paul lighting the lamps of Timothy and Titus, Priscilla and Aquila refining the ministry of Apollos (Acts 18:24-28). Rufus Jones called it "finding the *life clue*" within each of us.

For instance, as our group of young couples at Heritage Church began to grow, the need for marital counseling grew also. When the burden became too great for the pastor, the teacher of the young adult class was asked to share the task. The burden shared became a burden halved when she sensed it as her *life clue*. She enrolled in a family therapy course at a nearby state hospital and, after two years, became so accomplished at it that she was asked to join the hospital staff!

A pastor is one called to prepare his people for their ministries, thereby multiplying himself. He is not the *torchbearer;* he is the *lamplighter!* Second, he is to be . . .

The Pray-er for His People. When a pastor sees his primary role as a preparer of his people, it makes a difference in how he prays. He will stop praying for nebulous "revival" among his people and start praying for *persons* who, as Bruce Larson put it, will "dare to live now." He will stop praying for emotional responses from his people and start praying for effective inroads by them. He will stop praying for *more members* and start praying for *more ministers* — and thereby get both!

A vivid example of this was the coming together of three single young ladies in our Heritage circle. Until Kathy entered our Yokefellow group, the only single person was Sara. Never were two girls more different, but Sara was Kathy's only hope. Sara assumed it as her ministry and after a long cultivating friendship, Kathy yielded her "actual" for Christ's potential and became a Christian. Then came contact with Toni, whose background was so similar to Kathy's that there was no question whose ministry it should be. I began to pray for the appropriate time to bring them together. One Saturday Toni asked to meet me at the church office; during our talk, the climax of many previous conversations, I knew the time had come. I said, "There is a girl I'd like you to meet." My description of Kathy to Toni was interrupted, however, by a knock on my study door. *It was Kathy!* I was as shocked as Rhoda was when Simon Peter knocked at the gate (Acts 12:13-15), but it confirmed forever to me: the pastor is to be the *pray-er* for his people. Finally, the pastor is to be . . .

The Preacher to His People. When a pastor sees his role as the preparer of and pray-er for his people, it makes a difference in how he preaches. He begins to see Sunday not as a climax for the week just past, but a day of preparation for the week to come. There is a difference! The Jewish "day of preparation" is well worth borrowing and adapting. When the church week is spent getting ready for Sunday, it is usually spent in scolding (and scalding) the laity for what they did not do! But seen as a "day of preparation," Sunday becomes a time for strengthening and encouraging for the week to come. Dr. James Mahoney says, "The world has beat my people down all week; they don't need me to add to it, they need to be *lifted!*"

Job 4:4 in Moffatt's translation has been the motto for my pulpit ministry since first I read it. It is Eliphaz speaking to Job:

"Thy words have kept men on their feet."

In short, the pastor is the preparer of, the pray-er for, and the preacher to his people.

The great, but sluggish in the morning, Mendelssohn was awakened every day by a pupil whom he had instructed to play and keep on playing an unresolved chord on the piano. Mendelssohn could not take that! Thus every morning he arose and rushed to the piano to resolve the chord.

The great unresolved chord in the Church today is . . . *the ministry*. We must not rest until it is resolved.

Discussion Questions

1. Is the word "minister" usually a *noun* (a person) or a *verb* (an activity) to the group — and *why?*

2. Consider Dr. Haney's parody of "the ideal pastor" given in the chapter and his distinction between a "torch-bearer" and a "lamplighter."

3. In what practical ways can the group members discover their gifts and ministries?

Creative Group Procedure

When Christ saw "Levi," the tax collector, He saw a "Matthew" in him which merely needed uncovering. Allow the group to "see" each other by pointing out one another's obvious gifts. Emphasize that this does not mean to discuss what is "good" about each other or what we "like" in each other; the object is to point our obvious "gifts" which are, or can be, ministries to others. Individuals might also share what they believe to be their own gifts. Give attention to how the group can help one another develop their gifts.

To the Reader

At this point we make a transition. The previous chapters constitute a basic thesis. Be sure you grasp it — it is pivotal. The *kingdom* is the *goal*, the *Church* is the *agent*, and the *ministry* is for *all*. Review it. Live with it. Let it begin to use you. It is "The Idea of the Laity."

The remainder of the book is intended to be practical. These are the "ideas" stemming from "The Idea." I will explore ways of actualizing the Idea. Let it be stressed, however, that ministry — for a person or a congregation — is always personal and individualistic. These ideas are not to be borrowed or copied; they are meant to serve as a springboard for better, more personal, and local ideas. That's the idea of *The Idea of the Laity!* Read it, then, prayerfully and selectively. The One who is the Way has a way for you!

The Author

PART TWO

Chapter Four

Bible Study Selection

We left by ship from Troas and sailed straight across to Samothrace, and the next day to Neapolis. From there we went inland to Philippi, a city of the first district of Macedonia; it is also a Roman colony. We spent several days in that city. On the Sabbath day we went out of the city to the riverside, where we thought there would be a Jewish *place for prayer*. We sat down and talked to the women who gathered there. One of those who heard us was Lydia, from Thyatira, who was a dealer in purple goods. She was a woman who worshipped God, and the Lord opened her mind to pay attention to what Paul was saying. She and the people of her house were baptized. Then she invited us, "Come and stay *in my house*, if you have decided that I am a true believer in the Lord." And she persuaded us to go.

(Acts 16:11-15 TEV, italics added)

THE LAITY AND SMALL GROUPS
Fad or Function?

> *When I came into the silent assemblies of God's people, I felt a secret power among them, which touched my heart; and as I gave way unto it, I found the evil weakening in me and the good raised up.*
>
> ROBERT BARCLAY

The abrupt and spontaneous appearance of small groups throughout the kingdom of God today constitutes what Clyde Reid calls an "explosion." [1] Its unplanned-ness is seen in the fact that no denomination had either schedule or strategy for it and, to date, most have done little to implement it. This spontaneity bears all the earmarks of a moving of the Spirit — who usually operates from the Church's blind side.

While this phenomenon is writing a new chapter in the story of the Church, it is really not new. Small groups have been a part of our dynamic surges throughout Christian history. Christ's isolation of the Twelve from the throng was, in fact, a small-group movement. Indeed, there is evidence of even smaller groupings of the Twelve in the way they are listed in clusters in the gospels — most obviously the Peter-James-and-John circle. The small "house church" was an identifying characteristic of early Christianity (see Rom. 16:5). Lydia had a small prayer group under way at

---

[1] Clyde Reid. *Groups Alive — Church Alive.* (New York: Harper & Row, 1969), p. 15.

the time Paul arrived in Philippi (Acts 16:13-15), and the prayer meeting at Mary's house (Acts 12:12) must have been similar. Wesley's movement (Methodism) bore most of the marks of present-day small groups with home meetings, group prayer, and group disciplines.

THE POSSIBILITIES OF GROUPS.　What is really new are the proliferating possibilities presented to churches today via small groups. Renewal is predicated on the liberation of the laity for the work of ministry, and no method has yet proved more effective for it than the small group.

Evangelism.　Evangelism is properly both a message and a method. The message remains the same, but the methods vary. Currently we have two evangelistic methods, and both have relatively recent origins: revivalism and Sunday school. In many areas of the nation these are now beginning to wane and, as always, the Spirit anticipates and supplies our needs. The "new" is obviously the small group meeting in homes. [2] Reports of events bordering on the miraculous are filtering in from every quarter of the nation, indicating small-group success as a *method* by which the *message* can be delivered. Indeed, no less than Leighton Ford, a chief proponent of mass evangelism, says the small group is "the most promising focal point for evangelistic concern" today. [3]

Throughout Christian history, revivals and small groups have been like a pendulum, one replacing the other as it wanes in effectiveness, only to reappear later. Wesley was all but unique in that he combined both. The epigram introducing this chapter was the report of one in an early period and, in many cases, *could have been said* yesterday or today as the small group method again revives. In full, Robert Barclay (1648-1690) said:

[2] For help in starting an evangelistic small group, see: Ralph Neighbour *The Touch of the Spirit*. (Nashville: Broadman, 1972), Chapter 5; Girard. *Op. cit.*, Chapter 10; and Paul M. Miller. *Group Dynamics in Evangelism.* (Scottdale: Herald Press, 1958).

[3] Leighton Ford. *The Christian Persuader*. (New York: Harper & Row, 1966), p. 60.

Not by strength of arguments or by a particular disquisition of each doctrine and convincement of my understanding thereby, came I to receive and bear witness of the Truth, but by being secretly reached by this life. For, when I came into the silent assemblies of God's people, I felt a secret power among them, which touched my heart; and as I gave way unto it, I found the evil weakening in me and the good raised up; and so I became thus knit and united unto them, hungering more and more after the increase of this power and life whereby I might feel myself perfectly redeemed. And, indeed, *this is the surest way to become a Christian.* [4]

Bible Study. Often a corollary of evangelism, but not necessarily limited to it, is the use of the small group for more effective Bible study. It has some distinct advantage over our present method of Bible study, the Sunday school, in that it is (1) *informal,* usually meeting in a home; (2) *longer,* usually affording at least two hours of concentrated study instead of the 45-50 minutes of class time; and (3) *smaller,* thereby allowing for more group participation. Also, it often provides Bible study time for those unable to attend on Sunday, those who teach Children's classes, or couples who wish to study together when one or both are unable to attend regular classes.

Personal Growth. Many groups are formed for the express purpose of personal Christian Growth, both in knowledge and effectiveness. These groups usually study books other than or in addition to the Bible, moving from the devotional life to witnessing to doctrine. The ancient classics of Augustine, Thomas à Kempis, and William Law, along with more contemporary writers like Elton Trueblood, Keith Miller, Bruce Larson, Larry Richards, and Samuel Shoemaker, have proved effective in these studies.

Prayer. One of the richest contributions of the small group movement has been to revitalize *group praying* among Christians. These groups usually meet exclusively to pray.

---

[4] Quoted in: Samuel Shoemaker. *The Church Alive.* (New York: Dutton & Co., 1950), p. 101, italics added.

A brief portion of Scripture is read, requests are shared, and prayer follows. No one has contributed more to this resurgence of intercessory prayer than Rosalind Rinker, whose *Prayer: Conversing With God* has become a veritable handbook. [5] Most of these groups engage in some form of Miss Rinker's "conversational prayer" — that is, prayer does not "go around the circle" but takes place as a normal group conversation with Christ.

Tasks. The small group has also manifested great potential as a *task force* for Christian ministry and evangelism. Groups cluster around a need or ministry and many times add study to the agenda to learn how to serve more effectively. These groups visit state hospitals and rest homes, sponsor recreational programs, work with migrants, indigents, racial groups, the deaf, and other similar groups, interlacing witness with ministry. Both the Church of the Savior in Washington, D.C., and the West Memorial Baptist Church in Houston, Texas ("Touch" Ministry), are experimental churches using this idea as the basic organizational structure of the congregation. [6] Both congregations identify members with task groups, and both integrate their Christian education with it to correlate education with ministry.

Campus Ministry. Work with college students has been completely revitalized on many campuses by the introduction of the small group method. Dorm-groups and frat-groups provide the entreé for every sort of ministry on campus, from evangelism to study to task groups. Both denominational and interdenominational student groups use this method very effectively. [7]

Our campus ministry, primarily at the United States Naval Academy, centers on training key campus leaders who, in turn, conduct Bible study and Christian growth groups. We have also found this to be a productive method for reaching professors on campus. The strong witness on

[5] Rosalind Rinker. *Prayer: Conversing With God.* (Grand Rapids: Zondervan, 1959).

[6] O'Connor, *Call to Commitment;* Neighbour, *The Touch of the Spirit.*

[7] See: Keith Harris. *Working Creatively With Groups.* (Nashville: Southern Baptist Sunday School Board).

our three area campuses is the result of the small-group idea initiated by our student "multipliers." It is one thing to make a "mark" for Christ, which can be erased; it is something else to make a "marker" for Christ. Consequently, one fourth of our Sunday morning congregatian at Heritage Church is college students.

Therapy. While it requires professional leadership, some are using the small group for Christ-centered therapy. Family counseling has long been a scheduling problem for most pastors, and the group approach has promise as a needed timesaver at no loss of effectiveness; indeed, the evidence is beginning to indicate it is more effective and productive in many cases than individual counseling. Dr. John Drakeford has pioneered in this area with his Counseling Center at Southwestern Baptist Theological Seminary in Fort Worth. [8] It must be stressed, however, that this is a *professional* venture.

Market Place. The small group has often proved to be the "key" to entering the market place of daily work. There are prayer and study groups during coffee and lunch breaks in many factories and offices. "Dawn patrols" meet in churches or restaurants before the workday begins. One effective group for some of our Heritage men working in the nation's capital is a weekly luncheon group of office workers.

Youth. Willard Wild, our youth minister, uses the small group idea for programs of Bible teaching and Christian training with both junior high and senior high groups. It has the advantage over the usual "mass meeting" idea so prevalent among the older organized youth groups in that the evangelistic circle is also the discipleship circle.

Church Committees. Philip Anderson uniquely suggests that existing church committees and boards are "naturals" for renewal training: they are already a group and are usually small enough for it. [9] A portion may be added to the agenda of any committee with ease!

[8] John Drakeford. *Integrity Therapy.* (Nashville: Broadman, 1967).
[9] Philip Anderson. *Church Meetings That Matter.* (Philadelphia: United Church Press, 1965).

The amazing thing is . . . *it has just begun!* Time and prayer can only lead to the proliferation of the idea and the possibilities of small groups.

THE PROCEDURE OF GROUPS. How does one *start*, and *conduct* a group? John Casteel, who has contributed to the small group idea as much as any person, emphatically states:

> You cannot organize a group through a deliberate program. Groups come into being when the hunger, faith, and determination of concerned persons are matched with the leading and empowerment of the Holy Spirit. [10]

Just as the movement is His, *your* group must be, also. In nearly every case it appears a deepening hunger on the part of two or three erupts with a simultaneity bespeaking the ministry of the Holy Spirit. Groups are *born*, not *started*. Where to begin? Be the first member yourself and begin in a closet — the closet of prayer!

Experience has taught that those who wish to involve themselves gain a head start by taking time, individually or in a group, to study *group dynamics* before beginning. Careful distinction must be made here between group *dynamics* and group *techniques;* many times they are wrongly equated. "Techniques" are the various methods and procedures employed: room arrangements, the use of tools like pipe cleaners and the Quaker Questions. "Dynamics" is not something a group *does*, but what a group *has*. That is, there are processes through which all groups go, from leader domination to rejection; levels of communication; cycles; patterns; even ways of blocking the group process. There are personality patterns which emerge with regularity in all groups, and all groups work with an agenda of both ideas *and feelings*. Wisdom demands that an effective group or group leader be familiar with these dynamics which are unspoken guests. (Two good studies of group dynamics

[10] John Casteel. *Spiritual Renewal Through Personal Groups.* (New York: Association Press, 1957), pp. 191-92.

are Anderson's *Church Meetings That Matter* and Reid's *Groups Alive — Church Alive.*) Techniques are things groups do; dynamics, what groups have: the difference between *mechanics* and *dynamics!* Know it!

A study of techniques should follow. This includes the knowledge of how room arrangements add or detract; how the number of group members is chosen; and, especially, how the purpose of the group is decided. [11] That is, a circular room arrangement is best. Group size should vary between six and fifteen. A sharing group is better with six members, but a task group might require twelve to fifteen members to handle the particular mission adequately. A "group contract," mutually agreed upon, should be made at the outset as to the purpose of the group, meeting times and places, starting and ending times of meetings, agenda of each meeting (prayer, Scripture, discussion, etc.), and any common group disciplines required (daily prayer for each other, reading the book before the meeting). While these lessons require time, they are ultimately timesavers for those interested in using groups effectively.

The best place for a "common burden" is among one's own circle of Christian friends. Suggestion and mention might bring a telling response . . . or non-response. Trust the Spirit to lead you to others, pray about it in earnest, and share your desire with others. It will come; count on it!

For those interested in groups in *existing* churches, the "Heritage Plan" is provided in Appendix A.

THE PRINCIPLES OF GROUPS. While the effort at Heritage Church is at best an "interim report" after six years, we have discovered some principles worth sharing. Some of these we were able to anticipate by reading the reports of others, and some came out of our own experience. [12]

---

[11] Neighbour. *The Touch of the Spirit,* pp. 88-93.

[12] I am indebted to Bill and Diane Bangham, Bob and Colleen Giles, and Wanda Barker for isolating and identifying these principles which emerged from our group processes at Heritage Church.

1. The study of small group dynamics and techniques is the best thing we can advise before groups are launched. It solves many problems and immeasurably hastens the maturity of the group.

2. The object of renewal groups must constantly be kept before the group: to help one another be more effective. Two expressions are frequently uttered in our Heritage group. One is, "Let's lie down and play dead on that one"; it is used when a person raises a question more concerned with debate than encouragement. The other is the regular opening statement of each meeting: "We are here to help sharpen one another's swords, not to use them on each other."

A clearly defined and mutually accepted "group contract" can often preclude this kind of disruptive debate and, if it persists, a "group evaluation" form can be employed at the end of the meeting. This is a check-list evaluation of the meeting which deals with questions of leadership, communication, group warmth. Clyde Reid suggests a most usable sample: see Appendix B.

3. The idea of "ministry" must be repeatedly emphasized. The group are meeting to understand it, to discover their own, and to discipline it. Otherwise, the group becomes spiritually ingrown. Socrates taught that repetition is the first law of learning: keep the purpose of ministry ever before the group. Likewise, the discovery of "gifts" among the group members plays a major role in the group process. Two books extremely beneficial in this are Elizabeth O'Connor's *The Eighth Day of Creation* and Ralph Neighbour's *The Touch of the Spirit.* [13]

4. An atmosphere of openness and acceptance of each person in the group "as is" is the only climate in which there can be growth. At Heritage we well remember one couple who constantly challenged the group in argumentative fashion. The group reacted positively, however, and

[13] Elizabeth O'Connor. *The Eighth Day of Creation.* (Waco: Word, 1971). Neighbour. *Op. cit.*

when the couple later joined the church they gave this reason: the group had loved them *in spite of* themselves.

To create openness within the group nothing is better than the Quaker Questions. Each question is answered briefly by all before the next is asked: (A) *Where did you live between the ages of seven and twelve, and how many brothers and sisters were at home?* (B) *How did you heat your house?* (C) *Who was the warmest person in your life?* (D) *When did God become more than a word to you?* [14] The value of the questions is that as we share the usually intimate and often delightfully reminiscent answers, we open ourselves up to become known. Pipe cleaners are also a great ally. On one occasion, as we discussed the Christian home, each member was asked to bend the pipe cleaner into the shape of the "perfect marriage" and then to explain why. This was followed by the "perfect home" to include the children. It had an unusual opening-up effect upon the person as well as the group.

5. Groups should not be church- or denomination-related in a strict sense if they are to draw in outsiders. They should be groups in which most members "happen" to belong to the same church! Names like Yokefellows, Encounter Group, "Fish" Group, and CHUM implement this feature of openness. Yokefellow is a national organization [15] and CHUM, meaning "Christian Home Unit Meeting," is the group name used in the exciting Our Heritage Wesleyan Methodist Church in Scottsdale, Arizona. [16]

6. Ideas, tasks, ministries, or books should never be forced on the group. Let the Spirit lead. If the group is not sensitive enough to know the mind of the Spirit in unity, it is not ready for ministry anyway.

7. Stress that every member of the group must ultimately be responsible for other groups in some fashion. They are being *trained.* These outgrowths of leadership are the key

---

[14] See: Neighbour. *The Touch of the Spirit,* p. 93, on how best to use the Quaker Questions.

[15] Yokefellow Institute, 230 College Avenue, Richmond, IN 47374.

[16] See: Girard. *Op. cit.,* pp. 132-33.

to effectiveness. Some of the future groups they lead will involve drawing in or together other church members; others will involve totally new groups in their neighborhoods or places of work. Recently two of our Yokefellow One members initiated weekly lunch hour groups at their places of employment. Another Yokefellow "re-accepted" his call to the pastoral ministry, after avoiding it for a number of years, and enrolled in seminary. Within weeks we received a request from him for books and prayer support, as he had initiated a small renewal group on campus. It was not a surprise, however — we somehow expected it. Group *members* are supposed to become group *leaders*.

THE PROMISE OF GROUPS. There is much evidence that the small-group explosion heralds the long-awaited and prayed-for "awakening." Many who have prayed for such, however, have assumed that an awakening will be as it has been before. To them, "awakening" is a preconceived stereotype. James Burns's study of the great revivals of Christian history, *Revivals, Their Laws and Leaders,* is illuminating at this very point: every age which sought an awakening always sought it in terms of the previous one — and it was never so! [17] The only common elements to be found are (1) that it involves the laity, and (2) that it moves the Gospel outside the four walls of the church. The small-group explosion qualifies on both counts! Added to its favor is that it was unplanned and spontaneous, transcending denominational barriers. Its magnitude is not to be discounted, either. We could very well be on the . . . verge!

This is not to say it is without dangers and excesses; all awakenings have them. But the excesses have a way of "dying on the vine." Emerson vividly reminded us that there is a crack in everything God makes. The small-group movement faces the temptation of the bizarre, as with some of the "sensitivity" groups. [18] It also faces the excessive

[17] James Burns. *Revivals, Their Laws and Leaders.* (Grand Rapids: Baker, 1960), pp. 52-53. Originally printed in 1909.
[18] See: Jane Howard. *Please Touch.* (New York: Dell, 1970). A firsthand report on the sensitivity groups in the "Human Potential Movement."

aberration of the Tongues Movement. Most of all, however, the great danger is fad-ism. If groups lose their *purpose* (the cultivation and implementation of the lay ministry) and become the "in" thing — "let's have a group because First Presbapalian has one" — then it, too, shall die on the vine: *an aborted awakening!*

And, no sadder epitaph could be written to our generation than that: an awakening . . . *aborted* . . . because it became a *fad* without a *function*.

DISCUSSION QUESTIONS

1. Remembering that the purpose of the group is both positive and practical, openly discuss the various ways in which a group can become a divisive clique and the ways in which your group will guard against the possibility.

2. Which of the small-group possibilities seems to strike a responsive chord with the group members? This is not necessarily the decision to initiate such a group; indeed, the group needs to grasp the over-all concept of ministry first. But such can become a matter of group prayer as ministry is anticipated.

3. In what ways are the group sure that their meeting is *functional* rather than a mere *fad?*

CREATIVE GROUP PROCEDURE

If the group has not already done so, it should discuss and adopt a "group contract." If this has been done, perhaps it should now be reviewed and revised.

Using Clyde Reid's titles for various group personalities (like the "little tin god," the "porcupine," the "knight on a white horse"), let the group roleplay a group meeting on the topic of "Organizing a Bible Study Group." Assign various persons to play the roles of the "tin god" and so on. (See: Clyde Reid, *Groups Alive — Church Alive,* p. 50).

Chapter Five

Bible Study Selection

You then, my son, be strong in the grace that is in Christ Jesus, and what you have heard from me before many witnesses *entrust to faithful men* who will be able to teach others also.

Do your best to present yourself to God as one approved, a workman who has no need to be ashamed, *rightly handling the word* of truth. Avoid such godless chatter, for it will lead people into more and more ungodliness.

But as for you, continue in what you have learned and have firmly believed, knowing from whom you learned it and how from childhood you have been acquainted with the sacred writings which are able to instruct you for salvation through faith in Christ Jesus. All scripture is inspired by God and profitable for teaching, for reproof for correction, and for training in righteousness, that the man of God may be complete, *equipped* for every good work.

(2 Tim. 2:1, 2, 15, 16; 3:14-17 RSV, italics added)

CHAPTER FIVE

THE LAITY AND CHRISTIAN EDUCATION

To Equip or to Entertain?

> *We started by knowing that*
> *something was wrong.*
>
> JIM RAYBURN

Given the *idea* of the "laistry" — the ministry of the laity — as Christ's chosen strategy, the idea of Christian education increases in importance and takes on a new perspective: *to equip for effective ministry.* Teaching, learning, studying, and discipleship were all built into the structure of the God Movement from the very beginning. In some fashion or form, Christian education has been a primary element in the life of the Church in every age. In our time, it has been Sunday school. A rather recent method of Bible study, the Sunday school idea was initiated by Robert Raikes in 1780 in Gloucester, England. In the subsequent nearly 200 years, it has been refined and polished until it is the best organized and equipped Bible study method in history. Yet, it is here, in this the greatest era ever for organized Christian education, that we are ironically face to face with . . .

THE PARADOX OF CHRISTIAN EDUCATION. It is as uncanny as it is fantastic. With the best educational organization ever, with the best literature, curriculum, training, and

denominational support structures — all that we have produced is . . . a generation of biblical illiterates! One of the
most unsettling, unnerving experiences for any pastor, minister of education, or Sunday school teacher is to give a
simple test on biblical facts to a group of adults who have
been in Sunday school most or all of their lives! Whatever
we taught them, it didn't "take."

To add to the paradoxical agony, the chasm between
learning and doing is too wide to miss except for the blind
— the willfully blind. This gulf is the span between all we
should know and all that we are not doing: *the ethical vacuum.* Our "Bible Belt" was the heartland of prejudice, and
some of us in evangelical circles are only now discovering
that it is not a sin to feed the poor. And it's as obvious
as illiteracy and inconsistency that all the educational timber
we have piled on the fire has not really taught our people
how to *do* the Christian life, especially how to cultivate
their ministries. If the acid test is really fruit, not leaves
(as Jesus suggested in Matt. 21:18, 19), then we've got a
problem!

Now, however, with a full generation of experience behind us as data for examination, we can begin to sort out
some of the Sunday school shortcomings. The Uniform
Lesson Series idea, adopted or copied almost universally,
has now been used by a generation of students who failed
to learn in any lasting way. Where was the downfall?

THE PROBLEMS OF CHRISTIAN EDUCATION.   In brief, the
basic problem of the Uniform Lesson Series is that of *disconnected lessons.* We met and moralized over isolated
passages each Sunday, one week from here and next week
from there. Even the flurry of curriculum reform which
swept most denominations in the last decade was little more
than a new saddle for the same old dead horse — and the
results were the same. Our "add-ons" added nothing. No
matter how we approached it — from isolated moral passages to biblical themes, even studies of various books of
the Bible — all of them followed the same basic "skipping

around" pattern. Our best attempt to make it more comprehensive was the "greater lesson" which was to be read in addition to the "printed passage." But even while we encouraged it, it was requested with our tongues ceremoniously tucked in our cheeks.

The result? After a generation, most Sunday school graduates from the last generation's five- or seven-year "cycles through the Bible" believe there was a time in history known as . . . "Bible Days." It was a vaguely ambiguous period in which Abraham, David, Isaiah, and Peter were contemporaries. They all had the same world-view, fought the same enemies, believed the same things, and wore the same clothes. Bible Days were different in that, well, they were just different: miracles happened then and God spoke to people. Not like "nowadays." This is no carping criticism, however; it is the evaluation of most honest graduates of the system. It is hindsight, to be sure, but there was no other way to know if it would work than to try it — and, successful or not, it was far, far better than anything to date. But it has not been as effective as it could have been or can be.

If Problem Number One is *disconnected lessons*, then Number Two is the lack of purpose or, at best, a fluctuating one for Christian education. We were never clear on exactly what we were trying to teach students to *do* (or *be*, or *know*), and when we tried to clarify goals, we were general enough to hit any target. One young Ph.D. in Heritage Church said to me, "I now know the purpose of Sunday school. It is to produce Sunday school teachers!" His reasoning was based on the fact that a person stays in Sunday school until he is regular in attendance, and then he or she is given a class! Anyone in the house care to argue? And the implications of an in-house circular system are frightening.

The result of these two compounded problems was a third one: *competing functions* within the Sunday school. It slowly became the basic structure of most evangelical churches: it touched more of people more of the time than any other part of the church's life. Consequently, we began to *use* the Sunday school —

- it became an evangelism tool ("we can win to Christ three out of every seven new members enrolled");
- it became the organization through which we "promoted the budget" (a modern substitute for stewardship);
- it became the social unit of the church (though "fellowship" and *koinonia* are not quite synonymous);
- it became so much the focal point of everything we did that we even had to have a "general assembly" to make all the announcements!

Indeed, any *changes* made in the Sunday school came in the form of *additions* to the program; and, in the end, *education* suffered from a severe case of overloading. Like the cowboy who mounted his horse and rode off in all directions, we failed to reach any of the desired destinations. A writer for the research journal for the Baptist Sunday School Board (Southern Baptist Convention) says:

> Thoughtful people know that the typical Sunday school approach to Christian education has largely failed for all but the elementary ages — and perhaps there, too. It has succeeded in organizing, recruiting, enlisting, and expanding; but it has not educated people in Christian discipleship. And now both enrolments and attendance are in decline. [1]

This is not to say it is bad; Sunday school is a good idea! But it is not good enough. It can be better. In fact, it must be better . . . if the "laistry" is to be effective. And the place to begin, as Jim Rayburn says, is with knowing something is wrong. If we learn to label our problems "challenges," we have made a good start toward solving them.

THE PRINCIPLES FOR CHRISTIAN EDUCATION. Assume for a moment that we have a clean slate on which to develop

[1] Don B. Harbuck. "A Struggle for Creativity." *Search.* (Nashville: Baptist Sunday School Board, Winter 1972), p. 31. Used by permission.

a program of Christian education. There are no present programs or structures. What can we do? Step One is to establish a *purpose* for Christian education, and the following steps will grow out of it. I say:

> *The purpose of Christian education is to equip*
> *the people for their ministries in the world.*

If this is a valid basic premise, several implications become clear and become principles.

First, Christians need to understand the nature of their calling in the Christian life. One experimental church begins the educational process for all new members with sessions on how humans function spiritually. They look at conversion as a change in command. They examine the idea of the Holy Spirit being within the believer, along with all that He is to do and be to the follower of Christ. Another church requires its new members to take a course of study similar to that above and then give a public statement before the congregation on Sunday morning concerning their "spiritual pilgrimage" to date. [2] One cannot cultivate and nurture the Christian life until its purpose becomes clear.

Second, Christian education must provide a foundation of intellectual facts in addition to spiritual facts. There are some basic facts and ideas in the Faith which are necessary equipment, and one of our continuing problems is that we have made them intellectual luxuries instead of practical necessities. That is, an effective follower of Christ must have a basic knowledge of Old and New Testament history, doctrine, ethics, and church history. We tried to give these facts in the old system of lessons, but it lacked both the basic historical structure into which to fit the isolated facts and the pattern of historical continuity in study. When one enters seminary, he is required to take these studies, and it is done in a continued-study manner. If this is the proper way to teach in the seminary, why not in the local church?

2 These refer to the West Memorial Baptist Church, Houston, Texas (see its privately published "Touch Workbook"); and to the Church of the Savior in Washington, D.C. (see O'Connor, *Call to Commitment*).

If a minister (clergyman) needs these basics, why not the lay minister? Helen Khoobyar says:

> Introductory courses in the Bible and the basic Christian beliefs should be considered as a must in any program of adult education. They may serve as a starting point for the beginners and lead into more advanced and specialized courses. [3]

Foundational courses are intrinsic to Christian education, and it is not by accident or coincidence that, wherever renewal breaks out, the educational program inevitably reflects this pattern.

Third, the need for *functional education* is implied if our purpose is to equip for ministry. If the people have callings (and they do), and if these callings are as personal as the people (and they are), then the Church has the educational obligation to refine and equip. The people must be trained.

It is at this point, however, that we confront a major difference: the difference between *people-centered* and *program-centered* educational efforts. To be *program-centered* means that a church devises a program and then goes looking for people to fit into it. To be *people-centered*, however, is to discover the needs and desires of the people first and then to develop a program to fit both people and needs. At Heritage Church we have come to call the program-centered approach the "Cinderella Syndrome" — one size shoe has to fit everyone! The local church must become a *veritable shoe store* if the people of Christ are to walk the Way! The church exists to be an ally to the Christian, not the reverse! But so many churches are with their programs as Henry Ford was with his Model-T: "You can have it in any color you want, so long as it is black." This means we must add *breadth*, as well as *depth*, to the program of Christian education: it must be (1) spiritually interpretative, (2) foundational, and (3) functional in orientation.

[3] From *Facing Adult Problems in Christian Education*, by Helen Khoobyar, The Westminster Press. Copyright © MCMLXIII, W. L. Jenkins. Used by permission.

Therein lies the needed alternative to Christian education. But how? The fact is: we do not have a clean slate on which to work. We have existing structures and methods, and many believe these structures and methods to be sacred. One answer is to scrap all existing programs and start anew. In an established congregation, however, the results of this approach are predictable: the church will split! While some members may count this as evidence of spirituality on their part, it reflects a manifest callousness toward those who do not immediately see or agree with the need for change. Who is to blame for their static attitudes? The truth is: the church! *We* made them. Now we must take the responsibility of caring for them in an attitude of love. Robert Girard says of these traditionalists:

> These believers may be involved in the kind of church structure that stifles the sharing of life in Christ together, and inhibits spiritual growth. They may be all entangled in the red tape of the ecclesiastical bureaucracy that exists in many denominations. They may have prejudices, wrong ideas, and know nothing of dependence on the Spirit in any kind of practical, day-by-day way. They may seem to be almost mummified in the grave dressings of unbiblical church tradition. They may be opposed to anything that would disturb the status quo. But that doesn't alter the fact that if they have thrown themselves on Christ for salvation and He lives in them, they are a part of the Body of Christ. They cannot just be 'written off'! [4]

An existing congregation, if it is to exhibit *agape* love, cannot "halve" itself with a clear conscience. Thus the only alternative is to add the new to the old: a parallel program.

As the idea of Christian education, as opposed to church education, began to filter into Heritage Church by way of our Yokefellow groups, we found ourselves at the impasse which all existing-renewing churches face. When the impasse became too obvious either to ignore or to dismiss,

[4] Girard. *Op. cit.*, p. 182.

our response was to appoint a representative committee of twenty-five members to recommend a solution. The emphasis was placed on *representative* members: from all age and attitude groups in the congregation. Some were satisfied with the existing program, but they realized that other *loyal* members were not. These could not be labeled "troublemakers"; they knew each other too well for that. Others saw the need for change, but they also realized that the existing program apparently satisfied the needs of others. Thus our guiding principles were two: (1) to look at the educational needs of *our members* (not the church down the street or across the country) and (2) the kingdom of God idea (that God can bring diverse people together into a loving, working relationship) was a working possibility, not an ideal. We determined to "love a program into being."

We talked, asked questions, interviewed denominational leaders and experimental church representatives, argued and then prayed, prayed and then argued, and ultimately found a unity of direction. The result was a parallel approach of foundational studies alongside the regular Sunday school program.

The initial step was a two-year cycle of special studies which operated on the academic year, three quarters over nine months, the summer quarter being omitted due to vacations and their effect on the necessary continuity of study. Each person returns to his regular Sunday school class during this quarter.

YEAR ONE		
FIRST QUARTER (Oct.-Dec.)	SECOND QUARTER (Jan.-Mar.)	THIRD QUARTER (Apr.-June)
O.T. History	*Life of Christ*	*Life of Paul*
YEAR TWO		
Church History	*Christian Ethics*	*Doctrine*

Future studies are anticipated to grow out of the cycle, like studies in the Prophets or the Reformation. The two-year foundational program will be offered continuously in alternate years.

Several problems challenges immediately confronted us. The major one was (and is) with curriculum materials. These had to be inexpensive, and they had to be a balance between the too-simple and the too-complex. Indications are that both denominational and independent publishers are at work on these materials. Another problem/challenge was trained teachers. The first impulse was to ask the pastor to teach, but the Idea of the Laity took hold, thus it was suggested that the pastor equip some persons to teach!

We also made discoveries about the existing program. First, we learned the existing program and structures did, in fact, meet the needs of some, particularly the older members to whom this was familiar territory. It provided a security for them and a context which met many of their spiritual needs. Second, we discovered this need: since the foundational courses were built on the principle of continuity, there was no place for new members to "break into" the course once it was under way. The regular classes provided an alternative.

But above all, no matter how we approached it, we always discovered that the Sunday school *is* the basic structure of the existing church. It is the focal point for contact, for fellowship and age group activities which include both Yokefellows and others. Therefore, for the sake of records, all members are permanently enrolled in the regular Sunday school.

This program will most likely not be the *program* for any other church. At least it should not be. But it does represent a valid and workable *pattern* for *existing* congregations, as well as a measure of promise: it can be done without a division in the church. Regardless of the pattern or the program selected, however, the task of Christian education is to *equip* rather than to *entertain*. And it is "Unfinished Business" for the Church today.

DISCUSSION QUESTIONS

1. Carefully avoiding the possibility of negative criticism toward programs and personalities (since the nature of the group is always positive and practical), discuss the value of the Christian education the group members have received in the past. What elements were the *most* productive?

2. In what ways could the group's education become *foundational* and *functional?*

3. What *personal* studies and books may group members recommend to each other?

CREATIVE GROUP PROCEDURE

Imagine that the group members and their families are the nucleus of a new congregation. It is their responsibility to develop a program of Christian education for all ages. What will be taught and how? By whom in the group? Will it be done at church? at home? or both? What would be the major problems with the program, and how would they be handled? Is the finished product of the group a *workable* possibility?

Chapter Six

Bible Study Selection

With this in mind, then, I kneel in prayer to the Father, from whom every family in heaven and on earth takes its name, that out of the treasures of his glory he may grant you strength and power through his Spirit in *your inner being*, that through faith Christ may dwell in your hearts in love. With deep roots and firm foundations, may you be strong to grasp, with all God's people, what is the breadth and length and height and depth of the love of Christ, and to know it, though it is beyond knowledge. So may you attain to fullness of being, the fullness of God himself.

Now to him who is able to do immeasurably more than all we can ask or conceive, by the power which is at work among us, to him be glory in the church and in Christ Jesus from generation to generation evermore! Amen.

(Eph. 3:14-21 NEB, italics added)

THE LAITY AND THE INNER LIFE

Roots or Fruits?

> *Christ left the needy people*
> *in order to engage in prayer,*
> *not because He did not care,*
> *but because He cared so*
> *much that He had to have*
> *times apart for conscious*
> *communion with the Father.*
>
> ELTON TRUEBLOOD

The very title of Elizabeth O'Connor's volume, *Journey Inward, Journey Outward*, indicates the necessary balance which the follower of Christ must maintain. [1] If one is to demonstrate and spread the kingdom life, the spiritual reservoir must be fed by the "rivers of living water" which Jesus promised (John 7:38). Evelyn Underhill tells how an elderly Quaker widow once held her hand and said, "I hope, my dear, while you are watering souls you get a few drops for yourself!"

Of these two needs, the inner life and the outer, neither is the more necessary or important. Trueblood rightly says:

> If we neglect the roots, which are found in the life of
> silent waiting and common prayer, the fruits will soon

[1] Elizabeth O'Connor. *Journey Inward, Journey Outward.* (New York: Harper & Row, 1968).

wither and cease to appear. If we neglect the fruits, which are exhibited in the struggles against injustice, the roots become fundamentally sterile, and the resulting experience is largely self-centered. [2]

The temptation with which all of us constantly struggle is to unbalance them, consequently both must be constantly disciplined. Discipline, however, is tough business — much tougher than abstinence, which we would prefer for simplicity's sake. Frugality is always more difficult than poverty, and moderation than total rejection. But the balance required between roots and fruits will brook no such choice. Both must be nurtured — simultaneously. Yet, in an era like ours which stresses the fruits of Christian service, the greater temptation is to short-change the inner life. For that reason we must constantly review and revise our approaches to it.

How, then, does one cultivate the inner life? Consider five means as those most promising: (1) group life, (2) family life, (3) corporate worship, (4) group retreats, and (5) the personal devotional life. Since the first two of these are the subject matter of other chapters, we will focus on the latter three.

WORSHIP AND THE INNER LIFE. Perhaps the most overlooked and under-used resource for the inner life is the one most common to us all: corporate worship on Sunday. The purpose of worship is always the *encountering of Christ*, but quite frankly, in most evangelical circles it is usually for the *entertaining of Christians!* We go to "get something out of it"; we choose our hymns for melody rather than message; and we "enjoy" the sermon. Consequently, worship for most evangelicals is more akin to a short-lived *feeling in the heart* than it is to a *shot in the arm*, which might have some lasting influence upon us. We leave with a "glow on," to be sure, but not much to "go on." We see ourselves as the "audience" (notice the preference of "audi-

[2] Elton Trueblood. *The New Man for Our Time*. (New York: Harper & Row, 1970), p. 26.

torium" over "sanctuary" in evangelical circles) when, in truth, only One makes up the Audience in true worship.

There is a dangerous tendency in some forms of renewal which would replace corporate worship with dialogue, sharing times, and small-group study. While these are both needed and valid for renewal, they are not substitutes for worship. Many have wisely begun to employ these methods in an effort to revitalize the Sunday night service and give it meaning! Some, however, would wrongly replace all worship with such. There must be a time and a place when God is given *His say,* or we shall lose something unique to corporate worship.

Worship, rightly understood, is always a mystery and a miracle which "happens" when, and only when, we encounter God and feel ourselves *addressed* — which may not always be enjoyed! To worship in such a way that we are "encountered" requires us to see all the various facets of worship — singing, hymns, praying, reading the Scriptures, and proclaiming — as *potential avenues of communication* between God and the worshiper. Every hymn can become "my" prayer set to music. The pastoral prayer should always seek to gather up the requests of those present and be prayed in such a way that everyone present may silently say of some part, "Yes, that is my prayer, too." The reading of the Word should be a corporate experience of coming under the searchlight of the Scriptures together. [3] The sermon can become personal when a person earnestly prays for it to contain a personal message.

And, when we see and approach worship in this manner, time and time again the report is that — behind some line of a hymn, a sentence in a prayer, or a thought in the sermon — *Christ appears and addresses* "me." Then, and only then, is the inner life touched and tendered in such a way as to be outwardly productive in daily life. Try it — and then you will know what John meant when he re-

---

[3] One problem of corporate Bible reading in worship is the multiplicity of translations on the market today. Perhaps the idea of "pew Bibles" is worth considering for congregations.

ported: "I was in the Spirit on the Lord's day, and I heard behind me a great voice. . . . " (Rev. 1:10 KJV).

RETREATS AND THE INNER LIFE. The rediscovery of the retreat-for-advance idea is one of the most heartening elements of renewal, but it is just that — *a rediscovery* — for retreats are not new. They are as old as Moses on Sinai and as recent as Laity Lodge, Yokefellow House, and L'Abri. Think of Elijah alone on the mountain for forty days, Jesus in the wilderness with the Spirit — and the devil! — the frequent withdrawals of Jesus and His disciples, Paul in the deserts of Arabia, and even the Apostles on those days in the upper room before Pentecost. The Dominicans, the Franciscans, and the Jesuits have long employed retreats. Wherever renewal has cropped out, retreats have been an intrinsic element. Arnold Toynbee has noted that "withdrawal" has almost always been the preface to great advances throughout history. [4]

What is new, however, is the expansion of the retreat idea to include study and training in the Christ-life. (Our focus here, however, is on the deepening of the inner life. For those interested in the retreat idea for other purposes, a bibliography is attached as Appendix C) For inner life purposes there are two retreat possibilities: group retreats and the personal retreat.

The Group Retreat. The purpose of any retreat always determines its format. A retreat for cultivating the "inward journey" requires such possible elements as a speaker, a common book, discussion times, and times of silence (though a retreat need not have *all* these elements). With inner life retreats, the theme will focus on the ministry of the Spirit, the life of prayer, or perhaps the inner leadership of Christ; above all, it will be *practical*. A common error on such retreats, and one against which to guard, is to talk much about it but not to allow time in the schedule to do it! The "times alone" must be an integral part of the schedule.

---

[4] Arnold Toynbee. *A Study of History,* vol. 1. (New York: Dell, abridged edition, 1965), pp. 256-57.

An Anglican retreat guide, Father Andrew, says:

> I always say two things to those coming to a retreat. . . .
> We come to seek union with God. God is our quest.
> We are so liable to make a God of our own imagining,
> to seek ourselves in Him, to seek a God who will do the
> things we want Him to do. We have to learn to pray
> to the God who created us. "I pray to Thee as Thou
> art." We want to be alone with Him. Secondly, be-
> cause of that, the silence is important. We must not
> trespass on one another's privacy. If we saw two lovers
> together, we should leave them alone. Much more do
> we want to leave alone the soul that has come here to
> be with God. Let us try not in any way to intrude upon
> one another. [5]

There are many who will also attest to the value of a
common book to be read before or during the retreat by all
retreatants. Books like these have proved valuable on many
inner life retreats: Douglas Steere's *On Beginning From
Within,* Thomas Kelly's *A Testament of Devotion,* Dietrich
Bonhoeffer's *Life Together* and *The Cost of Discipleship,*
William Law's *A Serious Call to a Devout and Holy Life,*
Jack Taylor's *The Key to Triumphant Living,* Ian Thomas's
The Saving Life of Christ, Trueblood's *Company of the
Committed,* and Watchman Nee's *The Normal Christian
Life.* The author's *Renew My Church* and this present
volume are designed for retreat use, also.[6]

Times alone and group study-discussion should be bal-
anced not only by reading, but also by the "Emmaus Walk"
idea of two retreatants venturing off together to pray and
share with a "mysterious Third." The final session will seek

[5] Quoted in: Raymond J. Magee, ed. *Call to Adventure.* (Nashville:
Abingdon, 1967), pp. 39-40.
[6] Steere, *On Beginning From Within.* (New York: Harper & Row, 1964);
Kelly, *A Testament of Devotion.* (New York: Harper & Row, 1941); Bon-
hoeffer, *Life Together.* (New York: Harper & Row, 1954) and *The Cost
of Discipleship.* (New York: MacMillan, 1963); Law, *A Serious Call*
(various publishers); Taylor, *The Key to Triumphant Living.* (Nashville:
Broadman, 1971); Ian Thomas, *The Saving Life of Christ.* (Grand Rapids:
Zondervan, 1961); Trueblood, *Op. cit.;* Nee, *The Normal Christian Life.*
(London: Christian Literature Crusade, 1958); Haney, *Renew My Church.*
(Grand Rapids: Zondervan, 1972).

to bring to a climax all that the retreat intended. Forty-four hours invested in a weekend retreat on the inner life are far weightier in terms of spiritual enrichment than forty-four consecutive Sundays. It should be an annual part of every Christian's and every church's program; if renewal is the goal, it *must* be.

The Personal Retreat. The other leg to the Christ-walk within is the *personal retreat.* Sometimes as long as a week-end, sometimes as short as an afternoon, the earnest follower is constantly in need of getting away from all voices save the Voice. Christ often withdrew alone — sending the disciples ahead or leaving them behind. Sometimes it was only a stone's throw away, as in the Garden, but it was nonetheless *away*. "As was His custom" is too familiar an expression to miss in the gospel accounts of His prayer life. Anyone who would be an apprentice to the Carpenter must learn the value of the personal retreat in its relationship to the productiveness of service among the world's needy and suffering and seeking. Trueblood advises that "the discipline of each individual Christian should include some time alone each day, for a brief period, and longer times alone, perhaps once a month." He adds:

> Perhaps we need, once a month, a private retreat of at least six hours. This is not easy to get in modern life, that strange life in which timesaving devices seem to leave us less time, but we may be able to get it if we realize sufficiently how valuable it is. [7]

The goal of the personal retreat is the refreshing of the spiritual springs within, a reacquainting of our spirit with the Spirit, a re-examination of our life and call and, above all, just *to be with Him.* Herein lies the law of spiritual reciprocity which Jesus sought to teach His disciples: His call to and for them, as Mark states it, was (and still is) "that they *should be with Him,* and *that He might send them forth*" (Mark 3:14, italics added). Both are to be desired because both are demanded.

[7] Elton Trueblood. *The Yoke of Christ.* (New York: Harper & Row, 1958), pp. 136-37.

PERSONAL DEVOTIONS AND THE INNER LIFE. Besides worship and retreats, and perhaps more necessary to cultivating the inner life, is a period of daily, personal devotions including Bible reading, prayer, meditation, and devotional reading.

Bible Reading. Bible reading for the devotional purposes of feeding the inner life is vastly different from Bible study. The focus of the latter is *personal knowledge,* the focus of the former is *divine communication.* Devotional reading is prefaced with prayer and expectation that the same Spirit who inspired their writing can claim the words of the Bible again and address them to us. Amy Carmichael says:

> Have you noticed this? Whatever need or trouble you are in, there is always something to help you in your Bible, if only you go on reading till you come to the word God specially has for you. I have noticed this often. Sometimes the special word is in the portion you would naturally read, or in the Psalms for the day, or in Daily Light, or maybe it is somewhere else; but you must go on till you find it, for it is always somewhere. You will know it the moment you come to it, and it will rest your heart. [8]

Many have found that the Psalms, the gospel of John and the epistles are repeatedly "relivable" words. Others find Proverbs best, and still others find the historical narratives most productive. Whatever the choice, however, such reading should be followed by silence, a silence which Bonhoeffer calls "the simple stillness of the individual under the Word of God." We are silent, he says, "because the Word is still speaking and dwelling within us." [9] And, a rich legacy is forfeited if you fail to record *His-Your* word for the day in some form of prayer diary! [10]

Devotional Prayer. The one common directive in all the epistles, which shows its universal necessity, is the directive

[8] Amy Carmichael. *Edges of His Ways.* (Fort Washington, Pa.: Christian Literature Crusade, 1955), p. 41.

[9] Bonhoeffer. *Life Together,* p. 79.

[10] See: the author's *Renew My Church,* p. 53, for suggestions on a personal prayer diary.

to pray. It is in all of them. But never have we been more in need of praying, "Lord, teach us *how* to pray"! Knowledgeable inner life praying contains at least two basic elements: it is both *communication* and *communion*. Myron Augsburger, in as brief a definition of valid, victorious prayer as could ever be made, says:

> Prayer is not overcoming God's reluctance to act; it is opening one's life to God's willingness. Prayer is giving God the moral freedom to move in areas where He has wanted to but waited out of respect for the freedom of man. [11]

Communication involves both our thanksgiving and our requests. Above all, however, it must be personal. While "Thee" and "Thou" may have their place in formal public prayer, personal prayer is better off without them. Likewise, the idea of "saying your prayers" is as ludicrous as it is blasphemous in *personal* prayer. If we communicate with a person whom we love, we do not "say" a speech; we talk, we share, *personally*. Why not, then, with The Person?

Devotional prayer is also *communion*. By "communion" is meant that, often in personal relationships, we just want to be together with a friend and the topic of conversation is really inconsequential; indeed, conversation isn't even necessary. Just being together is an *end* as often as it is a *means* in prayer.

Inner life praying is usually and rightly concerned with "the sins of the spirit" (pride, anger, greed) rather than those of "the flesh," though these are necessarily involved. Our downfall in such prayer is usually that we do not go far enough for the cure. That is, we pray, "Help me to overcome pride" (or greed or whatever), but we fail to pray about what to overcome it *with!* A vacuum must always be filled, lest we chase out the resident demon but put nothing in its place . . . and it returns with seven others! (Matt. 12:43-45). One person I know prayed long and hard

[11] Myron Augsburger. *Faith For a Secular World.* (Waco: Word, 1968), p. 50.

to overcome greed and never did — until he learned that the only way to overcome it was to give away more money!

Another aid to effective inner life praying is the Iona concept of "the plotted day." That is, our praying becomes specific as we anticipate the events of the day before us and pray concerning our responses to them. While not all can be anticipated, much can be; our sensitivity to the Spirit during the events of the day is greatly enhanced when we have previously prefaced them with prayer.

Devotional Reading. An oft-missed vein in the mine of the soul is the use of the great devotional classics as a corollary to Bible reading and prayer. Such older books as Augustine's *Confessions*, Thomas à Kempis's *The Imitation of Christ*, Lancelot Andrews's *The Private Devotions*, Pascal's *Pensees*, Law's *A Serious Call to a Devout and Holy Life* and such modern books as Steere's *On Beginning From Within*, Fosdick's *Rufus Jones Speaks to our Time*, Trueblood's *The Prayers of Dr. Johnson*, and Keith Miller's *Habitation of Dragons* are of immeasurable worth. [12]

Trueblood says, "Nearly all of the classics of devotion have in common the conviction of the possibility and, indeed, actuality of the divine-human encounter." [13] Leonard Ravenhill has noted the chain of effect on one such classic, *The Life of David Brainerd,* the early missionary to the North American Indians who died a spent man at the age of twenty-nine. [14] William Carey read it and launched the modern missionary movement. Robert Murray McCheyne (whose own biography is a classic) [15] read it and swayed Scotland. Jonathan Edwards, in whose house Brainerd died, was deeply moved by it. Wesley said, "Let every preacher

[12] *Confessions, The Imitation of Christ, The Private Devotions, Pensees,* and *A Serious Call* are classics produced by many publishers; Steere, *Op. cit.;* Harry Emerson Fosdick, ed. *Rufus Jones Speaks to Our Time.* (New York: MacMillan, 1961); Trueblood, *The Prayers of Dr. Johnson.* (New York: Harper & Row, 1945); Miller, *Habitation of Dragons.* (Waco: Word, 1970).

[13] Trueblood. *The New Man for Our Time,* p. 65.

[14] Now out of print.

[15] A. A. Bonar. *The Biography of Robert Murray McCheyne.* (Grand Rapids: Zondervan).

read carefully the life of David Brainerd." [16] And the chain is yet to end — to Brainerd's *Life*, as well as the other classics — for what has been said of it could be said of all of them.

Yet the question concerning the personal devotional life is: "when?" The lives of those spiritual guides whose counsel is most valid and valued indicate that *the morning hours* are the best. George Washington Carver said: "All my life I have risen at four o'clock and have gone to the woods and talked with God. There He gives me my orders for the day." Elton Trueblood faithfully begins his day at 8:00 A.M. with Bible reading and prayer. Evelyn Underhill employed an hour each morning by dividing it into three twenty-minute segments for Bible reading, prayer, and then spiritual reading. Charles Simeon, the great English pulpiteer, devoted the morning hours from four until eight to devotions. John Wesley spent the hours between four and six in prayer, and Luther said, "If I fail to spend two hours in prayer each morning, the devil gets the victory through the day." Bishop Asbury, who gave American Methodism the character of an epidemic, also followed the pattern of two hours in the morning.

But how did they find the time? Trueblood is right when he says "the day is usually ruined the night before!" Only establishing priorities can free the time required.

This is not to say that nighttime is not the time for devotions, for nothing could be a more appropriate ending to the gift of another day. But it is to say that the weight of the devotional life should be borne in the morning. And the time? The more time one invests in service, the more he will need to pray; indeed, he will *have* to pray more, and he will *find* the time simply because he must. Trueblood is again our guide when he says:

> We, indeed, still have a little piety; we say a few hasty
> prayers; we sing meaningfully a few hymns; we read

[16] Leonard Ravenhill. *Why Revival Tarries.* (Minneapolis: Bethany, 1959), pp. 80-81.

snatches from the Bible. But all of this is far removed from the massive dose that we sorely need if we are to be the men and women who can perform a healing service in our generation. [17]

The *goal,* however, is the one thing we must not forget: the deepening and the quickening of the inner life *for outer service.* It is this alone which demands the cultivation of the spirit. Anything else is merely "hothouse" religion. It is to say with finality that roots and fruits can never be an either-or question. *Never!*

DISCUSSION QUESTIONS

1. In considering the cultivation of the inner life, discuss the group's strengths and weaknesses in the specific areas listed in the chapter.

2. Determine the part which committed self-discipline must play in filling and maintaining the inner spiritual life.

3. From personal experiences within the group, list some dangers encountered in stressing the fruits of the Christian life while leaving precious little time for cultivating the inner life.

CREATIVE GROUP PROCEDURE

Before the meeting, gather a sufficient number of *religious* papers and magazines, enough for each group member to have several. Also needed are scissors, glue, and a large piece of heavy paper or cardboard for each member. Let each member cut out words, phrases, and pictures from the papers and magazines and, by pasting them on the large piece of paper or cardboard, create a "collage" entitled "The Inner Life." This should include those elements necessary to an inner life. (Perhaps a sample could be prepared in advance.) Each one may then explain his or her work. These collages may be kept on permanent display in the meeting place.

[17] Trueblood. *The New Man for Our Time,* p. 66.

Chapter Seven

Bible Study Selection

Now we command you, brethren, in the name of our Lord Jesus Christ, that you keep away from any brother who is living in idleness and not in accord with the tradition that you received from us. For you yourselves know how you ought to imitate us; we were not idle when we were with you, we did not eat any one's bread without paying, but with toil and labor we worked night and day, that we might not burden any of you. It was not because we have not that right, but to give you in our conduct an example to imitate. For even when we were with you, we gave you this command: If any one will not work, let him not eat. For we hear that some of you are *living in idleness,* mere busybodies, not doing any work. Now such persons we command and exhort in the Lord Jesus Christ to do their work in quietness and to earn their own living. Brethren, do not be weary in well-doing.

(2 Thess. 3:6-13 RSV, italics added)

THE LAITY AND DAILY WORK

Life or Livelihood?

> *Through the Christian on the job the world meets the Church. But it meets far more: it meets the Divine Worker.*
>
> CARL F. H. HENRY

The Church has wrestled long, but never definitively, with the problem of Christian vocation and daily work. Are laymen "called" (the word "calling" comes from the Latin *vocatio* meaning "vocation"), or are only clergymen? Can daily work in the "secular" world be or ever become "sacred"? And, the pressing question, as we face the challenge of renewal of the Church today: how can the layman effectively *Christ-it* in the world of daily work?

The whole issue is seen differently at different times and by different strands in Christian history. This lack of a consistent pattern of thought only complicates the present challenge for lay men and women who want to integrate the Life with their livelihood. One of the earliest church orders (from Rome, ca. A.D. 197) rejects various vocations for believers: sculptors, painters, actors, charioteers, soldiers, magicians, and magistrates. [1] The Reformation opened the

---

[1] Henry Van Dusen, ed. *Christianity on the March.* (New York: Harper & Row, 1963), pp. 16-17.

doors of daily work as an avenue for service (ministry) to God and neighbor, largely as a rejection of the Roman view of clergy-only. Indeed, even today the *Catholic Encyclopedia* limits the term "vocation" to priests, monks, and nuns. The Reformation view of daily work was actually a spin-off from "the priesthood of believers" concept, but it nonetheless granted ministerial meaning to hitherto secular vocations. Fundamentalism modified both the Roman and the Reformation views by expanding "vocation" beyond the clergy, but also by limiting it so as not to include all professions. There is a lingering expression, "full-time Christian service," meaning church-related vocations, which indicates that a separation is still in effect in conservative religious thought. It is also interesting that evangelicals sometimes grant "calling" to certain other professions — i.e., school teachers and doctors — but most evangelicals would feel uneasy about thus labeling assembly line work.

The problem of rendering a contemporary verdict on vocation is further complicated by the meaninglessness of so many jobs in our present automated, technological world of work. There is little to suggest spirituality in many of the industrial responsibilities — pulling a lever or attaching clips for eight hours a day. Yet, when there is no alternative to such work, it must be *made* Christian by whatever spiritual and creative techniques the Church and the Christian can muster. Carl F. H. Henry is right when he says:

> If one is truly a believer, no boss and no machine can pluck him out of Christ's hand and thrust him into a morass of meaninglessness. Even monotony can be justified in the ministry of God and of humanity, if it stems from a constructive activity that has no better alternative. Whatever contributes to the elevation and good of mankind is worthy, even if it lacks romance and novelty. . . . Someone will say that this high response is more natural to the worker who deals directly with the persons who benefit from his labors, and this is true enough. But no worker's responsibility is lessened simply because he serves as invisible neighbor. Many a life has been saved by a properly tightened

screw, and many lost through an improperly tightened bolt. [2]

Indeed, many times the automatic routine and the regular breaks on the assembly lines afford more occasions for conversation and witness than on the office or sales end.

But whatever else the definition of vocation requires in our time, there are certain biblical "givens" and their implications which may be neither voided nor avoided. *One:* if we believe that God has a will and a plan for every life, then the will of God must logically include one's daily work. *Two:* if the will of God includes one's vocation, then one's vocation must be seen as a stewardship. Again Dr. Henry is our guide:

> A significant part of a Christian worker's witness is the quality of his work as well as the attitude toward his work. To say "I'm a soul winner, but I cobble shoes to pay expenses" is both right and wrong: while Christian witness is always a believer's responsibility, the work he does involves far more than a means of livelihood and carries tremendous spiritual overtones. That he make good cabinets and shelves is the very first demand that his religion makes upon the Christian carpenter as a worker.

> A photographer who takes poor pictures, even though he is an effective soul-winner, should either take his vocation more seriously, change his business, or at least confine his witness to non-customers! No impressive list of converts will offset a poor work record; one's work ought not to be of such questionable calibre that it disgraces God, discredits one's employer, and affronts society. [3]

Three: if one's work is in the will of God for his life, it intrinsically involves the responsibility of penetrating it for Christ. Granting these "givens" of the Faith, we can and must see our daily work as both a "calling" and a "ministry."

[2] Carl F. H. Henry. *Aspects of Christian Social Ethics.* (Grand Rapids: Eerdmans, 1964), pp. 59-60.
[3] *Ibid.,* p. 70.

But how does one arrive at this conviction of calling in his work?

YOUR VOCATION. A simple formula for testing one's sense of vocation which has proved helpful to many in the Heritage Church circle is: *Be in the right place, with the right perspective and with the right purpose.*

The Right Place. The immediate consideration for the layman in daily work is the question: is my present job in the will of God? Start there! Not — is it a good job, an honorable profession, or even an enjoyable one? But — is it for *me?* Bruce Larson reports of one man's struggle with this, and the conclusion reached is illuminating.

> I know a man who some years ago was a junior executive in a business. He had begun his Christian life by facing up to some failures in his marriage and family. After God began to work in his life by changing these basic relationships, he began to face his job. In a small fellowship group that met weekly for study and prayer, he said one night, "You know, I can't stay in my job. I'm being asked by my supervisors to do things that are dishonest. I'm low man on the totem pole, and I can't fight it. But as a Christian I can't be dishonest."
>
> We all prayed and for nine months he looked for a new job. He would have taken half the salary just to get out of that situation. But after months of closed doors, he finally said to the group, "I think I'm supposed to stay where I am and let God change the business through me." [4]

Thomas Mullen underscores this idea when he says that "men and women are consciously declaring themselves for vocations that *become* Christian simply because these people *make* them Christian." [5] On the other hand, it may be that the present job is not the right one. In that case, the task

[4] Bruce Larson. *Dare To Live Now.* (Grand Rapids: Zondervan, 1965), pp. 24-25.

[5] Thomas J. Mullen. *The Dialogue Gap.* (Nashville: Abingdon, 1969), p. 87.

of seeking the right one should begin immediately, and it should be faced with the confidence that the will of God is the only thing in the world of daily work that never goes wrong! He who is the Way always has a way.

The Right Perspective.   Once we have gained the sense of being in the right place, we should confront our perspective of the particular position: our attitude and grasp of our role. Bruce Larson suggests there are five questions which we should all periodically ask ourselves: (1) *Why am I here in this job?* Is it an accident or the will of God? (2) *For whom am I working?* For God or for men? You must "play it" to one or the other. (3) *What am I working for?* Wages? Prestige? To do the will of God? (4) *With whom am I working?* God's first concern is always "persons." He wants us to be aware of those about us. (5) *What kind of place am I in?* If Christ is serious about His revolutionary movement, then I am in a place of tremendous importance. [6]

The Right Purpose.   Primary among our purposes in daily work must be the conviction that we are placed in this world, and in our particular spot in the world, as "salt" and "light" (Matt. 5:13-16). When Jesus described Christians as salt and light, He did not say we *can be,* but we *are;* we are *all* the salt and *all* the light the world has! However salty we are, however penetrating our light, we are all of it there is. We are *it!* Whatever "salt" and "light" your place of work has, or is to have, will come from you. Remember your purpose! It is here that we face the really big question: "How do I *salt* and *light* my place of work?"

The *easiest way* that most have found is to start a Bible study or prayer group among the Christians or seekers in your office or factory. This can be done before work, during the lunch hour, or even as brief "one verse discussions" on the assembly line or during coffee breaks. This, however, raises another question: how do I identify myself and others as Christians or seekers to begin such a group? Many have found that by wearing a simple pin like the Yoke pin or

[6] Larson. *Op. cit.,* chapter 6.

Fish symbol, or by carrying a small New Testament in a shirt pocket, or by placing one on the desk, they can often create the occasion for such identification. Or, one may simply choose the bold approach which Keith Miller used in his office. With fear and trembling he publicly announced one Friday that he would begin a group before the workday began Monday. To his amazement, almost all fourteen employees in the office showed up! [7]

The *hardest* way to penetrate your place of work, and yet the most necessary one, is to live a complete transparent and Christlike life every day. And, when you fail at it — as fail you will — to rectify it with apologies. Sound tough? *It is!* This kind of life, in which Christ is felt to live again through you, is evidenced in many other ways, too. When we discussed this need in our Yokefellow Two group and later in one of our monthly Sunday night congregational dialogues at Heritage, the number one answer on both occasions was the same: one's *attitude* was most crucial. Much is said simply by how one relates to fellow workers, subordinates, superiors, customers, and the day-by-day problems which arise. Even how one gets angry — and sometimes it is necessary — reflects one's true life. The Christian is one who goes the second mile and whose motive for it is transparently Christlike. It is simultaneously an attitude of efficiency and empathy, of concern for products and persons, of personal love and professional loyalty. As Dr. Henry says: spiritual talk can never "be an excuse for shoddy craftmanship." [8] Even one's sense of business ethics is involved; more than one witness has been voided by a padded expense account! [9]

The *best* way, however, remains the one-to-one relationship of caring concern. One-to-one personal witnessing disallows any holier-than-thou attitude which may take stands but which destroys bridges. One must be open, if he would seek an opening for witness, and be ever sensitive to those

[7] Keith Miller. *The Taste of New Wine.* (Waco: Word, 1965), ch. 7.
[8] Henry. *Op. cit.,* p. 70.
[9] One of the few books available on Christian business ethics is Thomas M. Garrett's *Ethics in Business.* (New York: Sheed & Ward, 1963).

about him, as well as to the Holy Spirit who is always there to lead.

While the home is decreasingly a woman's primary place, it nonetheless holds forth a vocation for those to whom it is a calling — and a more noble one is hard to find. Dwight L. Moody was once approached by a mother with nine children who felt she was "called to the ministry." "Yes," Moody is reported to have replied, "and God has already given you your congregation!" However, all that applies in principle to those in industry and business, in terms of attitude and life-style, applies to the homemaker and mother, also; only the environment is different. Likewise, her relationship to other homemakers is an avenue of vocational witness, especially in her readiness to help, to care, and sometimes merely to listen. Some of the most effective evangelistic Bible study groups comprise homemakers who see the neighborhood as their mission field.

In the world of daily work, "vocation" is an option and "ministry" an obligation. The One who calls us to it knows; remember, He was first a *carpenter*.

YOUR OTHER VOCATION.   "Your Other Vocation," as Elton Trueblood called it, has to do with the investment of our gifts in addition to our daily work. To be "on duty" for Christ in the world of work entails but 32 to 40 hours of a week which contains 168. We are accountable for all of them. Here we refer to those ministries we perform in and through the churches.

The concept of the Church as the body of Christ, with each diverse part having a function, is an intriguing idea — and an exacting one. For the local church is just that: a collection of gifts — for the gifts which Christ gives in the context of the Church are *persons* with gifts! Each one is drawn by the Spirit into the whole for a distinct purpose. Some of these ministries are "inner" ones, like teaching; some are "outer" ones, like visiting. But how does one know what his or her ministry is? Often the body functions with only a few members actually working. Part of the problem is that only a few are asked, but to a greater degree it is that most have no sense for calling. *How does one know his ministry if none is obvious?*

Believe It. Christ has a ministry for you, a specific ministry uniquely yours. Believe it. Accept it as an assured fact. It may be greater than you anticipate or it may be less than you expect, but it is there.

Want It. A primary step in discovering the will of God in any life is wanting to know it and being willing to do it when it is made known. Jesus said, "If any man's will is to do His will, he shall know . . . " (John 7:17).

Pray About It. Begin to pray beyond the "request level" and seek the mind of Christ for your ministry. Pray that the Holy Spirit will lead you to it and that you will be sensitive to His leadership.

Ask About It. One of the best ways to begin discovering a potential ministry is to ask Christian friends whose maturity is obvious and whose judgment is trustworthy. Often our friends can see ministries in us to which we are oblivious.

Look for It. Often "a felt need," while it may not be the call, may at least be a clue. This was particularly true in my own call to the pastoral ministry: I *wanted* to preach! Yet, when I heard others relate how they had "fought" the call, I wondered if I had been correct. I was immeasurably helped by a professor who one day in class shared his call with the words: "I was not a draftee; I was a volunteer whom God accepted." That was me! Likewise, an obvious talent might be the clue. What do you have that may be invested in a ministry? One lady became concerned with the younger teenage girls in her neighborhood. She had been a trophy-winner with the baton in high school and was able to reach the girls with free baton lessons followed by a Bible study each week. A *felt need* and *an obvious talent!* Take an inventory of your assets; it may provide the clue. [10]

[10] Two extremely helpful books on discovering one's gifts are Neighbour's *The Touch of the Spirit* and Elizabeth O'Connor's *The Eighth Day of Creation.*

God has a way and a will for *each* of us — which can be known. Sometimes the *daily* vocation can be merged with the *other* vocation. A good example of this merger is Reid Hardin, an insurance man who saw the need for a retreat house and, with the help of friends, launched it along with a weekend program for church groups. Recently he was asked to initiate a renewal program for his denomination, the Southern Baptist Convention! But whether the vocations merge or not, only a sense of mission and calling can bring the wholeness of life which all of us seek. *Yours* is there, too! Emerson, in his essay on "Spiritual Laws," says:

> Each man has his own vocation. . . . There is one direction in which all space is open to him. He has faculties silently inviting him thither to endless exertion. He is like a ship in a river; he runs against obstructions on every side but one. . . .

DISCUSSION QUESTIONS

1. Determine the group consensus as to what makes a vocation "Christian."

2. Allow each group member the opportunity to make a private analysis of his life and livelihood in light of the statement, "Be in the right place, with the right perspective and with the right purpose." Sharing should be optional.

3. Discuss some of the group's preconceived ideas about "ministry" and "calling."

CREATIVE GROUP PROCEDURE

Let each member of the group list his normal daily work activities on one side of a piece of paper. In one column put a daily work schedule, including breaks and mealtimes. In a second column, list ways in which the Christian life might be integrated with the work activity, or ways in which the work activity is relevant to Christian service.

Chapter Eight

Bible Study Selection

Why all this stress on behavior? Because, as I think you have realized, the present time is of the highest importance — it is *time to wake up* to reality. Every day brings God's salvation nearer.

The night is nearly over; the day has almost dawned. Let us therefore fling away the things that men do in the dark; let us arm ourselves for the fight of the day! Let us live cleanly, as in the daylight, not in the "delights" of getting drunk or playing with sex, nor yet in quarreling or jealousies. Let us be Christ's men from head to foot, and give no chances to the flesh to have its fling.

(Rom. 13:11-14 *Phillips*, italics added)

Live life, then, with a due sense of responsibility, not as men who do not know the meaning and purpose of life but as those who do. *Make the best use of your time*, despite all the difficulties of these days. Don't be vague, but firmly grasp what you know to be the will of the Lord. Don't get your stimulus from wine (for there is always the danger of excessive drinking), but let the Spirit stimulate your souls. Express your joy in singing among yourselves psalms and hymns and spiritual songs, making music in your hearts for the ears of the Lord! Thank God at all times for everything, in the name of the Lord Jesus Christ. And "fit in with" one another, because of your common reverence for Christ.

(Eph. 5:15-17 *Phillips*, italics added)

THE LAITY AND LEISURE

Retire or Retool?

> *Time is what we want most but what, alas! we use worst; and for which God will certainly most strictly reckon with us, when time shall be no more.*
>
> WILLIAM PENN

It is paradoxically true that never have we had more time on our hands and never have we had less. We have not yet learned to adjust to our newfound leisure. Indeed, we are often too busy to realize that we now have an unprecedented amount of discretionary time!

In 1890 men spent an annual average of 3,300 hours at work. In 1964 the average had been reduced to 1,999 hours annually! Now we are beginning to see the 32-hour work week: an annual total of 1,664 hours. Some of these abbreviated work weeks are "four-day weeks," adding another whole day of leisure weekly. Honest calculation also requires us to substract those ten or so days sick leave; the two-, three- or four-week vacations; and the national holidays, most of them now rearranged for four-day weekends.

Equally true is that our leisure time is also more leisurely than ever. Time-saving devices for the home, the yard, and the garden have freed greater blocks of time. Increased transportation speeds must be included in our calculations, too — even though most downtown streets resemble parking lots at 5:00 P.M. every day!

Our response to this liberation has been another story, however. We have all but abdicated the control of our discretionary time to external forces. We kill time or fill it with second jobs, creature pleasures, adult toys, and assorted time-wasters. Failing to realize that killing time is but piecemeal suicide and refusing to discipline ourselves, we prove Bertrand Russell's aphorism correct: "To fill leisure intelligently is the last product of civilization."

For the Christian, however, time and its stewardship must be viewed from a different perspective. We are those who have "committed our lives" to Christ. But what is life? Life is *time!* "Our times are in His hands," it is true; but "our time" is not always so. This is not to say that the Christian response to leisure should be to add another worship service to the church week (though it would not hurt most of us) or that every waking moment should be invested in "church work" (which is not always the same as "the work of the church"). The most Christlike use of some free time often is absolute idleness. Jesus often withdrew from the crowds just to rest, and many times He urged His disciples to do the same. Mark records:

> And the apostles gathered themselves together unto Jesus, and told him all things, both what they had done, and what they had taught. And he said unto them, Come ye yourselves apart into a desert place, and rest awhile: for there were many coming and going, and they had no leisure so much as to eat. And they departed into a desert place by ship privately.
>
> (Mark 6:30-32 KJV)

Vance Havner says that when Jesus said, "Come ye apart and rest awhile," He really meant: "Come ye apart and rest awhile — *or come ye apart!*"

The very word "recreation" is illustrative: it means *re-creation*. But for most of us it is more like *wreck-reation!*

The word "leisure" is equally instructive in its etymology. In the Greek it is the word *schola,* from which we derive our word "school"; it evolved into our English language from the French *leisir,* the infinitive of which means "to be permitted."

Paul's instruction is perhaps more relevant now than when it was written: *"Redeem the time!"* It is more relevant if for no other reason than that we have more redeemable time than ever before. *But how?* The "why" we know; the "how" is the problem. Our need is to face the challenge *practically* in two ways. First . . .

LEISURE: Now. Most of us have huge blocks of time already on our hands: shorter work weeks, holidays, extended vacations — time which can be redeemed. The most needed area of investment for most of us is not the church. It is the . . . *home!*

The Home. Most fathers need to spend more time with their sons. So many of us are on the go so much that our sons are deprived of the only model of masculinity available. Most sons left entirely to their mothers seem to have a preference for lace. Mothers in the same way, need to spend time with their daughters. What we must see in the "hippie" life-style of so many youth is a *rejection* — a rejection of a work pattern whose bitter fruits they have had to eat and of a marital-family pattern apparently not particularly appealing. Communes are nothing more than a substitute and nothing less than a rejection.

Equally so, couples need to spend more time together, apart from the children. The husband-and-wife relationship is prior to children and superior to it. When children enter the circle, the tendency is to make them the hub rather than the spokes. Yet when they leave, the husband-and-wife relationship is still there. But when the relationship has not been maintained and nurtured during the child-rearing years, there is nothing left when the children go. *Except divorce.* How many marriages of twenty-years-plus do you know which did not make the transition?

The Self.   Another needed investment of leisure is time alone with ourselves. How seldom any of us is ever *alone!* And when we find ourselves alone, often our reaction is to flip on the radio or television or to grab a book or the paper. The prayer of one such hurried (spell that "harried") soul was:

> Slow me down, Lord!
> Ease the pounding of my heart
> By the quieting of my mind.
> Steady my hurried pace
> With a vision of the eternal reach of time.
> Give me,
> Amidst the confusion of my day . . .
> The calmness of the everlasting hills.
> Break the tensions of my nerves . . .
> With the soothing music of the singing streams,
> That live in my memory.
> Help me to know
> The magical restoring power of sleep.
> Teach me the art
> Of taking minute vacations of slowing down
>   to look at a flower;
>   to chat with an old friend or make a new one;
>   to pat a stray dog;
>   to watch a spider build a web;
>   to smile at a child;
>   or to read a few lines from a good book.
> Remind me each day
> That the race is not always to the swift;
> That there is more to life than increasing its speed.
> Let me look upward
> Into the branches of the towering oak
> And know that it grew great and strong
> Because it grew slowly and well.
> Slow me down, Lord,
> And inspire me to send my roots deep
> Into the soil of life's enduring values
> That I may grow toward the stars
> Of my greater destiny. [1]

[1] Author unknown.

The Church. The Christian, however, must inevitably face the challenge of free time and the Church. One's ministry is paramount, and the new time afforded to accomplish it is ever there, either to condemn or to challenge us. Time is there for equipping ourselves through training and study; and time is there for engaging in ministry.

The answer lies in the better budgeting of our time. And *budgeting* is the precise word we need to employ. More and more, the mark of spiritual maturity in our time is the grace and grit to discipline our schedules.

Most of us, however, operate under what must be called "the illusion of freedom." That is, the reason we usually give to justify our refusal to budget time is that we want "to be free and flexible" to do the most important things as they arise. This is an *illusion* simply because we are free to do those things most important *only* as we discipline our time. An athlete is free to become an athlete only as he disciplines himself, and a writer as he deliberately schedules writing times. It is also an *illusion* of freedom in that most of our so-called unexpected interruptions can really be anticipated. They are really whims!

If we would strive for mastery, then blocks of our time must be *committed* to Christ, times at which we "report for duty." An evening here, a day there, a weekend, a holiday — committed to Christ. (Indeed, the word "holiday" is but our paganized contraction of "holy day.") To redeem the time means the same as it does to redeem the soul or the life: it means to save it, to convert it — for *Christ's* use. Second . . .

LEISURE: THEN. Another form of leisure has recently become available: the pregnant possibilities of *retirement*. A reservoir of unlimited talent and expertise only awaits a channel provided by the Church. Seventy percent of those over sixty-five in America are now unemployed (especially by the churches!). And they are a "better" sixty-five than ever before, too.

But the half has not been told until we say that the challenge is to be even greater with the prospects of earlier retirement. By 1985 fully 21.2 million people will retire between the ages of fifty-five and sixty-four. Most industrial plants now have the "thirty years and out" retirement plan in effect, regardless of age. (One man I know, employed by a General Motors division, will retire this year at the age of fifty-two!) The military also retires after twenty and thirty years. One can only touch the hem of imagination's garment as to the potential for Christian ministry among and by this group.

Most in this group are physically healthy, mentally keen, and financially independent. Businessmen could become church business managers; teachers could become religious education directors; there is no reason why there could not be a complete retooling for a person to a church-related ministry in any area. Most of it could be done with little or no remuneration by the churches since most of these persons already have adequate retirement income.

Widowhood, though a sad lot, is nonetheless a reality, and a growing one. Women are living at least seven years longer than men: a ratio of 74.6 years' average to 67.1 for men. Their lives could have new meaning if the churches would but provide training and opportunity.

Heretofore, our thought has been to entertain these able-bodied and willing men and women. But why not equip and engage them in ministry? Lyle Schaller says:

> Instead of planning programs for older people that will occupy their time and fill up the hours in a lonely day, the new call is to help these individuals find new and meaningful roles in life. One of the most creative responses in this direction is in those parishes which invite persons with free time to share in carrying out the ministry of the church. Instead of viewing these persons as an object of ministry, they are asked to become partners in ministry. [2]

[2] Lyle E. Schaller. *Impact of the Future.* (Nashville: Abingdon, 1969), p. 39.

"For the committed Christian," Elton Trueblood says, "retirement means not an introduction to nothingness, but liberation for service." [3]

The opportunities are there, but there are also accompanying implications if the *retired* are to become the *retooled*.

Personal Implications. The first need is to see the need and become conscious of the stewardship of time afforded us in the retirement years ahead. Each Christian should begin now to pray and plan and prepare for it. Trueblood says:

> If this idea is to be effective, we must begin preparation for liberation long before it occurs, because, if we wait, it may already be too late. That the idea is beginning to catch on is deeply encouraging. Recently, a man said, half-jokingly, "I am going as a missionary to Florida." Whether the freedom from toil, which modern technology makes possible, is a blessing or a curse depends, in large measure, upon the pattern of thinking about ourselves and our vocations. It is here that the Christian faith can make some of its most potent contributions. The man who always wanted to be a missionary, but could not do so, he thought, because of the demands of family and secular occupation, may bring deep meaning to his mature years by volunteering to engage in work for which there is no financial support. Assuming good health, which is increasingly experienced after the age of retirement, new and hitherto unsuspected avenues may open. [4]

If it is time to begin thinking about retirement *money*, it is time to begin thinking about retirement *ministry*.

Denominational Implications. If we are to view this possibility with a seriousness that goes beyond Senior Citizens Clubs, Golden Agers, and chores around the church, then the denominations must provide pre- and post-retirement training for Christian service for the laity. That they are

[3] Elton Trueblood. *The Validity of the Christian Mission.* (New York: Harper & Row, 1972), p. 88.
[4] *Ibid.*

beginning to see the potential is seen in the new opportunities afforded retirees by missionary boards; but the idea is far too big to be contained within a single area.

The seminary is the real place of ministerial training and, if the ministry is opened to the laity, then so must the seminary. Innovation will be required, of course, but it must be done. Shortened, one-year preparation courses for retirees going into church-related vocations (directors of education, recreation directors, business managers) will be needed. Short-term and evening courses could provide pre-retirement training. Urban T. Holmes states:

> My plea is then, *first of all*, that we recognize that many seeking to fulfill a ministry in the Church are in fact persons with a charismatic gift, capable of functioning creatively as liminal figures, and that we design for them an education that particularly meets their needs and makes no pretense at being professional training. . . .
>
> What would be the purpose of seminary for them? Formation seems to be the obvious answer. A B.A. degree would only be required of those who upon entrance wanted to combine Christian formation with training in some profession such as social work, library science, graduate study in education, etc. The seminary curriculum would be designed to last only nine to eighteen months, and it would consist largely of courses intended to give understanding of the commitment the candidates already felt. Training in spirituality (the prayer life, patterns of Christian discipline, the writings of the mystics, etc.) would necessarily lie at the heart of what I am suggesting here. . . . [5]

The denomination can become the ally of the Christian seeking to add to the cause with the investment of its lives and of the churches which exist to support both laymen and denomination. In many ways this could be the rebirth of the denominational idea among the laity, and there is no doubt about it: how the denominations respond to this challenge will indicate clearly *who exists to support whom!*

[5] Holmes. *The Future Shape of Ministry,* pp. 268-69.

Church Implications. Finally, the local congregation has the dual function of *encouraging* the idea of retooling the retiring and of *employing* the retooled when they become available. One can but imagine the liberation this may bring to beleaguered staff members; what new ministries may be opened up heretofore impossible due to the lack of time and leadership; and what fresh ideas may be incorporated into the life of the churches by these creative people. It is true that, in some cases, the church will have to aid in the financing of the retooling of some, but what better investment (with dividends) of church money could there possibly be? Yet the local church is the key to it. It is both the start and finish to the project: it must *call out the called* and then *employ the equipped* when they are ready.

The hour is as late as it is great. But the risks — especially the risk of apathy — are also present. The failure of the church and the denomination to tap this reservoir will be a great one. But the greater loss will be to the individual retiree who fails to grasp his own potential and rocks or golfs away his better years. That possibility makes the words of T. S. Eliot even more haunting:

> In the land of lobelias and tennis flannels
> The rabbit shall burrow and the thorn revisit,
> The nettle shall flourish on the gravel court,
> And the wind shall say: "Here were decent godless people:
> Their only monument the asphalt road
> And a thousand lost golf balls."

DISCUSSION QUESTIONS

1. To allow the groups to see how they spend their time, ask each member individually to "chart out" an average day of his life (include work, sports, church, TV, going to and from work) and an average weekend.

2. In light of the chapter, each group member consider the statement, "I am disposably His." Discuss what de-

mands such a statement may have on a person's life if adopted as his.

3. In view of the group's Christian involvement, discuss the possibilities of retooling the retired church member and the possibilities of ministry such retooling could afford their church.

CREATIVE GROUP PROCEDURE

Let the group members suggest various and personal ways in which leisure time could be well employed by the group as a whole and as individuals. Someone should write these on a chalkboard (or something similar) under the two headings of "Leisure Now" and "Leisure Then," the latter referring to retirement. Each member should then choose and state the "one most needed" in each column. Practical ways of beginning such use of leisure should then be discussed.

Chapter Nine

Bible Study Selection

But will God dwell indeed with man on the earth? Behold, heaven and the highest heaven cannot contain thee; how much less this house which I have built! Yet have regard to the prayer of thy servant and to his supplication, O Lord my God, hearkening to the cry and to the prayer which thy servant prays before thee; that thy eyes may be open day and night toward this house, the place where thou has promised to set thy name, that thou mayest hearken to the prayer which thy servant offers toward this place. And hearken thou to the supplications of thy servant and of thy people Israel, when they pray toward this place; yea, hear thou from heaven thy dwelling place; and when thou hearest, forgive.

(2 Chron. 6:18-21 RSV)

Do you not know that your body is a temple of the Holy Spirit within you, which you have from God? You are not your own; you were bought with a price. So glorify God in your body.

(1 Cor. 6:19, 20 RSV)

THE LAITY AND CHURCH BUILDINGS

Dedicated "To" or "For"?

> *The only place Jesus failed*
> *was inside a building.*
>
> JESS MOODY

It is avant-garde today among the spiritually elite to view church buildings with scorn. They speak of "authentic house churches," an "Old Testament throwback," and, of course, the "edifice complex." What they fail to see, however, is that church buildings were born out of need; that, while we have been wrongly at times building-*centered*, we have always been building-*related*.

The early Christians held a twofold relationship to buildings in the dawn of the movement following Pentecost. That is, they continued to maintain a relationship with the local synagogues with which they were affiliated, and they apparently gathered in homes for "Christian" meetings, also. The early Christians wanted to keep their Judeo-Christian lineage intact, for the Faith is indeed a direct descendant of Judaism. Thus Peter and John regularly went to the Temple for the Jewish hours of prayer, as in Acts 3, but they also shared in "Christian house fellowships" as with the upper room and Mary's house (Acts 12:12). The Apostle Paul apparently started his ministry in each city at the synagogues; in fact, when he departed on the trip to Damascus which led to his conversion (Acts 9:1-9), it was to "the synagogues" he was going to look for those of the Way (Acts 9:2). The truth is, Christians left the synagogues only because they were forced out of them!

Pushed out of the synagogues as they were, the house church idea was the Christians' only option. The "church building" concept emerged in the major cities where there grew up several (in some cities, many) house congregations. A central place, a "headquarters of the company," became simply a coordinating necessity. It is true that the headquarters building did not materialize until somewhere between the third and fourth centuries, but this was not by choice of the Christians; it was against the law for them to build. Since then, however, buildings have been an integral part of the Christian strategy — one blessed of God. Whether or not they are valid or needed today is another question, to be sure, but it remains that the idea was born of need.

THE PERIODS OF CHURCH BUILDINGS. If we are to assess the validity, the need, and the use of church buildings today, we must consider the past. There have been six discernible building relationships in our covenant history.

1. *The Tabernacle.* The Tabernacle was a portable tent initiated during the wilderness wandering period immediately following the exodus from Egypt, and it was used until the Temple was built in Jerusalem. Thus the Israelites used it for three hundred to five hundred years, depending on the debatable date of the Exodus. The Temple dates from the reign of Solomon, which began about 970 B.C. The Tabernacle was viewed as (1) the "dwelling place" of God (the noun "tabernacle" comes from the Hebrew verb "to dwell") and (2) the symbol of His presence among the people.

2. *The Temple.* When the people of God were settled in the land of promise, and later united under King David, it "was in the heart" of David to build a temple in Jerusalem. This dream, however, was to be fulfilled by his son Solomon. The Temple was viewed as was the Tabernacle: the dwelling place of God and the symbol of His presence. That the Temple was the "dwelling place" of God was understood, though, as being less than literal. Indeed, Solomon said at its dedication: "But will God indeed dwell on the earth? Behold, heaven and the highest heaven cannot contain thee; how much less this house which I have built!" (1 Kings 8:27). But *proper theology* is not always the same as *popular opinion,* and most of the people viewed it rather literally as the dwelling place of God. Solomon's Temple was destroyed during the invasion of 587 - 586 B.C. Zerubbabel rebuilt it after the Jews' return from Babylon, completing it in 517 - 516 B.C., though not so superbly as Solomon. A third one, Herod's Temple, was begun in 20 B.C. and was still being constructed during Christ's lifetime.

3. *The Synagogue.* The idea of the synagogue, though apparently present in embryonic form from the time of Moses, materialized during the *exilic period* following the destruction of Jerusalem and the Temple in 586 B.C. The word means "assembly" or "congregation." To the people, being away from the Temple was all but the same as being away from God. Synagogues were initiated as local substitutes for the Temple and, while intended as a temporary measure, they became so integral to their religious lives that the idea was retained after the Exile ended. They were viewed as houses of prayer, of worship, and of religious education. The synagogue marked a distinct transition from the Tabernacle-Temple concept: the synagogue was more the *gathering place* of the people than the *dwelling place* of God. Most cities and villages in Palestine had one, Jerusalem had several, and the Jews who lived outside the Holy Land had them, as in Thessalonica (Acts 17:1) and Berea (Acts 17:10) in Greece.

4. *The House Church.*   As noted above, the house church
of the early Christians emerged first as a companion to
the synagogue and ultimately as the only place of meeting.
Someone's home in each city was used for worship, for education, for prayer and fellowship — much after the pattern
of the synagogue. The word *ekklesia,* which we translate
"church," literally means "the called out," and it implies
an assembly of people called together. This was the meeting arrangement for several centuries for Christians and
lasted until the laws prohibiting church buildings were
lifted.

5. *The Lord's House.*   The next step was the church
building, the name implying a return to the Old Testament
view of the dwelling place of God. The word "church"
evolved from the two Greek words *Kyrios* ("Lord") and
oikia ("house"). While we use "church" to translate *ekklesia*
("the called out"), it is a wrong usage; "church" is a de-
rivative of the Lord's House idea. As early as the beginning
of the fourth century there were forty basilicas in Rome,
and with the reigns of Constantine and Theodosius the
building period flourished. [1] As time passed, however, these
buildings became more elaborate with each succeeding
period: from Romanesque to Gothic (which added stained
glass) to the Renaissance revival of classical Greek architecture. They slowly ceased to be gathering places of the
people and became "the Lord's Houses." These buildings
became more and more like monuments to God than meeting places for His people. Indeed, some of them were built
not for use but for viewing. In many ways it was a step
back for the Church.

6. *The Meetinghouse.*   So long as there was a "Christen-
dom," a united church, as in the Middle Ages, the buildings
had a uniformity. The Reformation, however, brought
changes, especially among the more insurgent groups. The

[1] J. G. Davies. *The Origin and Development of Early Christian Architecture.* (New York: Philosophical Library, 1953), pp. 15-16.

mainline Reformation groups simply "took over" the Roman church buildings and, with minor alterations, used them without problem. For instance, the Lutheran reformation began in 1517 - 1520, but the first Lutheran church house was not erected until 1543. [2] The other Reformation groups, mostly Anabaptist, were too radical even for the reform leaders and, consequently, they were forced to return to the "house church" idea for their meetings. As these groups enlarged and matured to the point of erecting their own buildings, they maintained the meetinghouse idea with simple buildings reflecting a theological perspective disallowing any concept of the buildings being "dwelling places of God."

The term "meetinghouse" was popularized by George Fox, the founder of Quakerism, and was used by other dissenting groups like Baptists, Brethren, and Amish. (The cornerstones of both the first Baptist church in America, in Providence, Rhode Island, and the College Avenue Baptist Church, forebearer to our present Heritage Baptist Church, bear the word "Meetinghouse.") In contrast, Fox called the other buildings "steeple-houses." His report of the discovery of this difference reads:

> At another time it was opened in me that God, who made the world, did not dwell in temples made with hands. This, at the first, seemed a strange word, because both priests and people used to call their temples or churches dreadful places, holy ground, and the temples of God. But the Lord shewed me, so that I did see clearly, that He did not dwell in these temples which men had commanded and set up, but in people's hearts: for both Stephen and the apostle Paul bore testimony, that He did not dwell in temples made with hands, not even in that which He had once commanded to be built, since He put an end to it; but that His people were His temple, and He dwelt in them. [3]

[2] Andrew Drummond. *The Church Architecture of Protestantism.* (Edinburgh: T. & T. Clark, 1934), p. 20.

[3] *The Journal of George Fox.* (London: Dent & Sons, Ltd., 1924), p. 7.

Five years later, in 1651, he wrote:

> Now the Lord had shewed me, while I was in Derby
> prison, that I should speak in steeple-houses, to gather
> people from thence; and a concern sometimes would
> come upon my mind about the pulpits that the priests
> lolled in. For the steeple-houses and pulpits were offen-
> sive to my mind, because both priests and people called
> them the house of God, and idolised them; reckoning
> that God dwelt there in the outward house. [4]

This same view now holds sway among those who seek
the renewal of the Church. It is interesting to note how
carefully the expressions "meetinghouse" or "headquarters"
are used among renewalists. They recognize that a church
is *people* who meet in a *meetinghouse.*

THE PROSPECTS OF CHURCH BUILDINGS.   Now we are ready
for yet another step in our relationship to buildings. We
have passed through, and theologically beyond, the dwelling
place to the meetinghouse. Our present need is to express
that the building is also a place *from which we go* as well
as a place to which we gather! A new terminology is thus
required, one which reflects both the times and the ministry
of the laity. When Elton Trueblood led the dedication
services for our new Heritage Church facilities in 1972,
he suggested two such terms, to which I have added a
third.

The Armory.   To employ a military metaphor, perhaps
most appropriate in Annapolis, Trueblood suggests we must
view our buildings as places where we come to be *armed*
for combat (see Eph. 6:10-17) and *equipped* for service.
Not only are we to *meet,* we are to *muster!*

The Launching Pad.   Trueblood's other metaphor is an
apt one, for it emphasizes that the church building is also
a place *from which* we are to go. One of Dr. Trueblood's
favorite stories is of a man who unknowingly visited a silent

4 *Ibid.,* p. 49.

Quaker meeting. After sitting awhile, he asked one of the Quakers: "When does the service begin?" The memorable reply was: "The service begins when the worship ends!" The meeting together is never the *end* of meeting, it is a *means*. All of us are far more Sabbatarian than we would admit; we view the Christian day of worship as the *end of the week* rather than the *first day of a new week* of service! The Lord's Day is not a climax! It is a day of preparation! Leonard Griffith says:

> We had better be realistic and face the fact that in our generation the Church is not a crowd of people pouring into a shrine to make up an audience for a popular preacher or a recital of sacred music. In our generation the Church is a small company of Christian soldiers trickling out of the shrine to fight the battles of the Kingdom of God where men live and work and play and make decisions. In a lecture delivered at the City Temple in November 1963, Dr. Thomas Jessop, one of Britain's leading philosophers, said, "We shall not persuade a nation that has become widely secularized in two generations to put its affairs into a deeply decent order (still less convert it to our faith) by merely talking at it from self-enclosed sanctuaries. Our doors must be open as much to let folk out as to let them in. . . ."[5]

A Service Center. Not only is the contemporary church building to be a meetinghouse, an armory, and a launching pad — a place to which *we* come and from which *we* go; it must also be a place to which *others* may come. It is to be a seven-days-per-week activity center, existing to meet the needs not only of members, but of the community as well. As Sam Jones used to say, "The church is not so much a rest home for saints as a hospital for sinners!" Day-care centers, recreation areas, senior citizen's meetings, ad infinitum, give the building a mission and a ministry.

If we are to make this needed transition beyond the meetinghouse successfully, we must, then, realistically face . . .

[5] Leonard Griffith. *Encounter With Christ.* (New York: Harper & Row, 1965), p. 54.

THE PROBLEMS OF CHURCH BUILDINGS.   Eric Hoffer hit the nail right on the thumb when he said that "no one really likes the new; we are afraid of it." [6] Perhaps that explains the title of his book: *The Ordeal of Change*. One poetic wag expressed it thus:

> Our fathers have been Churchmen
> For nineteen hundred years or so;
> And to every new suggestion
> They have always answered, NO!

The Architectural Problem.   The most obvious hindrance to such multipurpose use of our buildings is current church architecture. While it is usually beautiful, it often does not lend itself to . . . *use*. Indeed, most building designs begin with the *exterior appearance*. Any use therefore, is required to fit the limited possibilities of an outer design. Building planning should begin with purpose. This purpose, in turn, should be determined from a twofold perspective: the needs of the members and the needs of the community. Concerning the latter, the community around the building should be surveyed for existing and anticipated needs. Are there a number of senior citizens in the area? Is there public housing with many children nearby? Are there a lot of footloose teenagers? Is it an inner city area needing a used-clothing dispensary? Having first viewed the needs, we can determine a purpose and then prepare a design. Not the reverse.

The exciting possibilities available today in church building are vividly portrayed in the stories of the Church of the Savior in Washington, D.C., and the West Memorial Baptist Church in Houston, Texas. Both made the transition from ostentation to ministry, the former using a large, older mansion and the latter, a service-oriented building. [7]

---

[6] Eric Hoffer. *The Ordeal of Change*. (New York: Harper & Row, 1952), p. 3.

[7] See: Neighbour. *The Seven Last Words of the Church;* and O'Connor. *Call to Commitment.*

Heritage Church in Annapolis was forced to relocate in 1970-'71; it built along functional lines, all rooms being multipurpose, without interior load-bearing walls, to permit later renovation. Renewal concepts played a major role in the planning, with a large, open fellowship hall to allow for a variety of uses and a lounge with a fireplace to provide a home-like setting for groups. (See Appendix D.)

One church recently built motel-like sleeping rooms into its new building to make the church into a retreat center! When buildings are built *to be used*, they usually are.

For existing buildings the choices for change are limited, of course, but they *can be made* — if a ministry presents itself! Whenever the "new" has struck in church history, architecture has been altered to fit. The Reformers redid their church buildings, and the Puritan movement in England also resulted in architectural change.

> Hooper, Bucer, and Ridley were convinced that the medieval two-roomed church (with nave separated from chancel by rood-screen and arch, as well as by steps) was fundamentally unsuited to Reformed worship. The Church of England had inherited such buildings, yet it was convinced that the true liturgical unit was not the clergy, with the laity as onlookers, but the whole body of the faithful gathered at worship. Even the larger parish churches had insufficient space for vast gatherings of the people, since much of the space was taken up by chantry chapels, and the choir intervened between the nave and the altar. . . . [8]

In Strassburg, Bucer moved the altar around to face the people and ultimately replaced it with a pulpit. Hooper, in England, replaced the stone altars with wooden tables. In both instances the idea was *mobility and flexibility* of building use. [9] When a reformation comes, buildings must be re-formed, too.

[8] Horton Davies. *Worship and Theology in England, 1534-1603.* (Princeton, New Jersey: Princeton University Press, 1970), p. 362.

[9] *Ibid.*, pp. 363-64.

The Theological Problem.   The central theological problem with giving our buildings a ministry is the lingering Lord's House heresy among us. It was and is a throwback to the Temple idea: pre-Christian at best and pagan at worst! This was brought home to us recently at Heritage Church when we bused some ghetto children into our Vacation Bible School, most of them never having been in a church house. One little six-year-old pointed at me as I walked by and asked her teacher: "Is he God?" Further questioning revealed she had made the association from my leading the daily worship service "in God's House"!

As George Fox reminded us, the *only* temple (dwelling place) of God is *the heart* of a believer. "Ye are the temple of the Holy Spirit" (1 Cor. 3:16; 6:19, for example) is the message of the *New* Testament. The problem which the Lord's House idea produces is that such buildings are *dedicated to God* instead of . . . *to God's use!* They are then *shrines* rather than *servants, monuments* rather than *ministers.* Buildings "dedicated to God" have a way of becoming "too sacred" to use. I know of one family who left a church because it served monthly fellowship dinners, basing their decision on an erroneous interpretation of 1 Corinthians 11:22 — not realizing that "church" does not mean a building, but "people." Indeed, Trueblood reminds us:

> We smile, sometimes, at the church supper, but we are not wise when we do so. *It is the oldest Christian ritual.* [10]

Moreover, when a building is "too sacred" to use, I think God would just as soon give it back to us! A building is *too sacred . . . not to use!* (See Appendix D.) Just prior to this writing I was co-host for an East Coast "talk show" with a representative of a major magazine. He told of a church located next to a school for the mentally retarded which had no playground. The pastor suggested to the vestry that the church lawn be used, but they rejected the

[10] Elton Trueblood. *Alternative to Futility.* (New York: Harper & Row, 19..), p. 71.

idea. The pastor then turned to this magazine's foundation, which bought an adjacent lot and provided the equipment at the pastor's request. Who? *Playboy!*

The Economical Problem.   Instead of becoming a way to minister, many times buildings can be *in the way* of ministry — if the amortization of the debt takes all the available money! Many churches now commit one-third or more of their incomes toward debt, to the exclusion of serving. In 1971 alone, churches spent $813,000,000 for new buildings in the United States. Assuming that half of this money was borrowed at 6 percent interest (a most conservative estimate), interest alone required $24,390,000! Perhaps this could be justified if the buildings were utilitarian, but the unspoken truth is that much of it went for sheer *ostentation.* To be sure, we have the example of Mary: her breaking the alabaster box of ointment to anoint Christ when (as *Judas* said) it could have been used for the poor; but Jesus approved of Mary. Yet there are limits to some of our applications of this unique episode. Clarence Jordan sermonized it once by saying:

> A church in Georgia just set up a big $25,000 granite fountain on its lawn, circulating water to the tune of 1,000 gallons a minute. Now that ought to be enough to satisfy any Baptist. But what on earth is a church doing taking God Almighty's money in a time of great need like this and setting up a little old fountain on its lawn to bubble water around? *I was thirsty . . . and ye built me a fountain."* [11]

If we are to implement the new with the old, our buildings must be seen in a new light. They are places to which we go, for sure, but they are also places from which we are launched and to which others in need may turn. Our "problems" — architectural, theological, and economical — are really "challenges" to both our *ingenuity* and *spirituality.*

[11] Lee, ed. *The Substance of Faith and Other Cotton Patch Sermons by Clarence Jordan,* p. 19.

Buildings labeled "Dedicated *to*" instead of "Dedicated *for*,"
in today's world, deserve a further label: *Ichabod!*

> I suppose I've passed it a hundred times,
> But I always stop a minute
> And look at the house, the tragic house,
> The house *with nobody in it!*

DISCUSSION QUESTIONS

1. Of the six building relationships we have had in our
   covenant history, discuss which is the most typical of
   our attitude today.

2. How does the group react to the concept of the church
   building being "The Armory," "The Launching Pad,"
   and "A Service Center"?

3. Have several group members read and report on the in-
   novative use of church buildings by such groups as The
   Church of the Savior in Washington, D.C., West Me-
   morial Baptist Church in Houston, Texas, and Heritage
   Baptist Church of Annapolis, Maryland (see Appendix
   D).

CREATIVE GROUP PROCEDURE

Let the group imagine that the house or the church building in which they are meeting is situated in the following
location; discuss ways of using the home or building to minister to such a community. A city of 100,000 people sur-
rounds the building or home. Nearby is a public housing
project of 1,000 people, mostly welfare recipients without
male leadership in the home. Adjacent to it are a private
subdivision of upper-middle-class homes and an apartment
complex for senior citizens. About one mile away is a state
college with mostly black students living in dormitories.
Because an extraordinary sales corporation is located in the
city, there is a large group of post-college-age single people
who have to travel on weekends and cannot attend regular

church services. A newspaper series has recently disclosed widespread use of narcotics at the local senior high school.

In what ways may the building or home be used (not a hypothetical facility, but the one in which the group is now meeting) to minister to this city? What groups need help the most? What needs may not be met due to lack of facilities? What may be done to alter the building to minister to these groups?

You wives must learn to adapt yourselves to your husbands, as you submit yourselves to the Lord, for the husband is the "head" of the wife in the same way that Christ is head of the Church and saviour of his body. The willing subjection of the Church to Christ should be reproduced in the submission of wives to their husbands. But, remember, this means that the husband must give his wife the same sort of love that Christ gave to the Church, when he sacrificed himself for her. Christ gave himself to make her holy, having cleansed her through the baptism of his Word — to make her an altogether glorious Church in his eyes. She is to be free from spots, wrinkles or any other disfigurement — a Church holy and perfect.

Men ought to give their wives the love they naturally have for their own bodies. The love a man gives his wife is the extending of his love for himself to enfold her. Nobody ever hates or neglects his own body; he feeds it and looks after it. And that is what Christ does for his body, the Church. And we are all members of that body

For this cause shall a man leave his father and mother, And shall cleave to his wife; and the twain shall become one flesh.

The marriage relationship is doubtless *a great mystery,* but I am speaking of something deeper still — the marriage of Christ and his Church. In practice what I have said amounts to this: let every one of you who is a husband love his wife as he loves himself, and let the wife reverence her husband.

Children, the right thing for you to do is to obey your parents as those whom the Lord has set over you. The first commandment to contain a promise was:

Honor thy father and thy mother
That it may be well with thee, and that thou mayest live long on the earth.

Fathers, don't over-correct your children or make it difficult for them to obey the comandment. Bring them up with Christian teaching in Christian discipline.

(Eph. 5:21 - 6:4 *Phillips,* italics added)

THE LAITY AND FAMILY LIFE

Misery or Ministry?

> *If honesty and purity be not
> in the heart, they are not in
> the home: and if they are
> not in the home, they are
> not in the City.*
>
> T. S. ELIOT

In our efforts to demonstrate and spread the kingdom of God, we often overlook the most obvious place of need: *the home*. It is the most obvious, the most needed, but also the most . . . difficult! Bruce Larson aptly subtitles his chapter on the home in *Dare to Live Now* as "The Acid Test." [1] Dwight L. Moody once said in a remark which needs no explanation: "Show me a person who is a Christian *at home* and I will show you a *Christian!*"

It is, however, one thing to say and quite another to do; one thing to set our minds to it and another, our hands. But that we do it is "must" business — for those who would take Christ and the Christ-life seriously. This is true simply because of the crucial role of the family in the life of the individual and in society itself. The individual innately craves what the home alone can provide: acceptance, love, security, and a sense of worth. These can be gained from other sources, but the home puts them all together in one

---

[1] Bruce Larson. *Dare To Live Now*, chapter 3.

place. The home is also a microcosm of society. It is where we learn how to live together, to discipline ourselves and each other in a context of love and acceptance; the place where basic family patterns are learned and adopted. The contemporary family must see the current youth rejection of accepted family patterns — like premarital sex and communes — not as an alternative or a new pattern, but as a *rejection!* And, to the would-be Christian home, it is both a threat and a warning.

But how does one *Christ-it* in the family circle? How does one demonstrate and spread the kingdom of God? How is the Kingdom *actualized* in this most needed place? If it is done, it will be done within the framework of three basic relationships.

HUSBAND AND WIFE. The primary relationship in the home, and in society as well, is that of a man leaving his father and his mother and cleaving unto his own wife, a union in which the two become "one flesh" (Gen. 2:24). It is the *hub* of life — and the *rub!* As a pastor involved in pre- and postmarital counseling, I find myself having to say basically the same things over and over again. There must be something basic and common to us all; there are lessons we all must learn. We must learn to . . .

Live Together. The basic problem is that, as Kenneth Foreman says, to take a husband or a wife is "to take the only sort of person with whom you can never fully sympathize." [2] We are different sexes and different sorts! "All marriages are 'mixed marriages,'" Harold and Charlotte Clinebell remind us;[3] we bring differences together and propose a unity of diversity which baffles the best of us. We marry each other, but we also marry each other's families and life-styles. It is inevitable from a "structural" standpoint that families are involved, simply because the basic

[2] Quoted in: George E. Sweazy. *In Holy Marriage.* (New York: Harper & Row, 1966), p. 3.

[3] Harold J. and Charlotte H. Clinebell. *The Intimate Marriage.* (New York: Harper & Row, 1970), p. 182.

grasp of what mates are and are to be is learned from our parents. Adjustments have to be made when the gears do not mesh. Ogden Nash expressed it in a humorous vein with which most can identify:

Just as I know there are two Hagens, Walter and Copen,
I know that marriage is a legal and religious alliance
  entered into by a man who can't sleep with the window shut
  and a woman who can't sleep with the window open. . . .

Moreover, just as I am unsure of the difference between
  flora and fauna, and flotsam and jetsam,
I am quite sure that marriage is the alliance of two
  people, one of whom never remembers birthdays and the
  other never forgetsam,
And the one refuses to believe there is a leak in the
  water pipe or the gas pipe, and the other is convinced
  she is about to asphyxiate or drown.
And the other says, "Quick, get up and get my hairbrushes
  off the window sill; it's raining in," and the one replies,
  "Oh, they're all right; it's only raining straight down."
That's why marriage is so much more interesting than divorce,
Because it's the only known example of the happy meeting
  of the immovable object and the irresistible force.
So I hope husbands and wives will continue to debate and
  combat over everything debatable and combatable,
Because I believe a little incompatibility is the spice of life,
  particularly if he has income and she is pattable. [4]

But it isn't always funny — as any pastor knows or, for that matter, any husband or wife! We have *to learn* to live together.

We must learn that we marry persons, not a "set of qualities." [5] There is good and bad, acceptable and unacceptable, in both partners. We accept each other "as is." To initiate a marriage with the latent idea of changing the other is bad business — and usually a bad bargain. Like a used car, we take each other "as is," willing to accept the implications and hidden problems.

[4] "I Do, I Will, I Have" by Ogden Nash, *The Ladies Home Journal*. May, 1948, lines 1-2, 5-8 omitted. Copyright, 1948, by Curtis Publishing Company. This poem originally appeared in the *New Yorker*.
[5] George E. Sweazy. *Op cit.*, p. 23.

In marriage we take another person whose happiness in life is solely our responsibility. Happy marriages do not "happen"; they are "made." It means that the other's happiness is a thing carefully calculated and planned. Compromise is as much a part of it as are flowers and new slippers! We, then, start with a fundamental challenge: we have *to learn* to live together.

Grow Together.   Learning to live together means, in turn, learning to grow together. The person we marry is not the same person five years hence; or ten years, either. We grow . . . inevitably; and, if we grow and change, we must learn to do it *together*.

A recurring problem of couples is that they do not make allowance for this process of maturation and change. Yet our concepts of the ideal home, the ideal house, even our life and marriage goals, change. They are different at age twenty-one, age twenty-five, age thirty-five, and so on. We are always in transit. The Clinebells list eight chronological stages in marriage.

> Stage 1: Courtship and engagement
> Stage 2: Wedding to beginning of first pregnancy
> Stage 3: Parents of preschool children
> Stage·4: Parents of school children (ages 6 to 13)
> Stage 5: Parents of adolescents (ages 13 to 19)
> Stage 6: Parents of children leaving home
> Stage 7: Empty nest to retirement
> Stage 8: Retirement to death of one spouse. [6]

In each stage new relationships emerge, sometimes abruptly. Thus it is mandatory to anticipate change and remain flexible. We are continually blessed with a new husband and wife all along — *a polygamous monogamy,* and each new mate affords the delight of falling in love again.

Talk Together.   Another recurring need is communication. Often a marriage is shaken at the outset because "the" topic of conversation has now materialized — "getting married" — and there is nothing left to talk about! Learning

[6] Clinebell. *Op. cit.,* p. 105.

to talk together, necessary to both living and growing together, largely depends on common interests and shared activities. Otherwise we are left to one-sided conversations.

Communication is also needed to meet problems effectively and resolve them. Couples must learn to express (and accept) freely when irritations arise. I am continually amazed that when adultery occurs, the couple usually stays together! Separation comes when a thousand little things pile up and, most of the time, the couple cannot put their fingers on the problem. The problem, of course, is communication. Unexpressed problems breed! Paul gave us a great principle when he said, "Never go to bed angry — don't give the devil that sort of foothold" (Eph. 4:26, 27 *Phillips*). Aileen and I kiss and say "I love you" every night of our marriage before going to sleep. While we have had to grit our teeth a time or two hundred, it keeps the lines open and reminds us continually that our love supersedes our problems.

Pray Together. To "pray together" is a catchall meaning that the spiritual dimension to marriage is all-important. Marriage is God's idea, not Adam's; it is foolish to try it without Him. And the most important spiritual element is not often seen. It is not attending church together, though this is expected. It is not to read the Bible and pray together, though the values of this are not to be underestimated. The most important element is *for a couple to keep pace* with each other in their spiritual growth. When the pace is out of balance, the common ground and bond so necessary to spiritual union disappears because the couple are at different levels of maturity. This is why churchgoing and Bible-reading together are *no guarantee* of a good marriage. Going to church, shared devotions, and other activities are necessary, but they are tools to keep pace with each other; therein is their value. Talk and discussion of spiritual concerns must be added to the other elements.

Having seen so many church marriages go sour, I cannot say it enough: *keep pace!* Learn to live *together,* to grow *together,* to talk *together,* but most of all to pray *together.*

PARENT AND CHILD. The same four elements also hold true in the second basic relationship in the home: parent and child. This, too, is a process of learning to . . .

Live Together. In the family context a child learns how to relate to others, to relate in various levels and, in turn, to relate to himself. How to relate to authority is learned in the parent-child relationship and to peers in the brother-sister relationship. The developmental years are the irrevocable home years. This is why *positive, explained* discipline is necessary, as well as the matter of having to share. How a grown-up child relates in his work to authority figures, even to the law, and how he relates to peers at work — indeed, to all of society — finds its roots in home relationships. Many current problems with the "generation gap" stem from seeds planted a decade or two ago. These are but the logical fruits. A parent honors his stewardship of the gift of a child when living together is a planned effort of responsibility before God.

Grow Together. A child's physical growth is natural; a child's maturity is not. The parent is responsible to provide the context in which maturity may flourish. This means, not that we "mold" the child, but that we allow the child "to become" the person God intended. Many conflicts between parent and child are but skirmishes over this boundary line — molding or becoming. Frustrated parents attempting to live their lives through their children inevitably produce both parental and juvenile frustration; it is just a compounding of the problems. Elizabeth O'Connor writes:

> One of the reasons we experience so much difficulty with our gifts is that parents have thought their chief function in life to be feeding, clothing, and educating the young. However, their really important ministry is to listen to their children and enable them to uncover the special blueprint that is theirs. [7]

Care, then, must continually be taken to *know* a child and each is different — and then to maximize his potential.

[7] Elizabeth O'Connor. *The Eighth Day of Creation*, p. 18.

For a child to know that he is not a disappointment is a vital handle on life. The child grows, and interests both flare and fizzle; but a drift is there — a God-given one. A parent has a God-given responsibility to cultivate a child's God-given personality.

Talk Together. Most of us talk "at" our children rather than "to" them. We fail to view them as little *persons*, little persons with opinions, ambitions (however fleeting), problems, ideas — all of big concern to them. They need to share them and we need to know them. One father I know holds a regular conference with his two-year-old-son while shaving each morning — to the great delight of both. I have found a periodic luncheon date with my sons a good thing for each of us. I often take others to lunch — why not them? They enjoy it, too!

Parents often confess after a child's episode with the law or some similar problem, "I had no idea" or "I didn't know. . . ." Communication channels opened early stand a far greater chance of staying open later. An *atmosphere* of openness must prevail, however. Children must feel free to introduce any subject and discuss it intelligently. When nothing need be hidden, nothing usually is. Talk to your children! This is especially true with a growing spiritual awareness in their lives.

Pray Together. For the Christian household, however, nothing takes precedence over the spiritual responsibilities. Most Christian parents attempt to set the right example by taking their children to church and to church-related organizations, and this is important. What they frequently fail to convey is the degree of importance. That is, when church is "skipped" for a Sunday, what is it skipped *for?* A value judgment is made by the child by simple comparison. This is often true of his Sunday offering; he receives a dollar for this and for that, and a dime to put in church. Again, an attitude of value is conveyed.

Likewise, six days and twenty-three hour each week in the home either reinforce or invalidate the one hour at church. Perhaps the most frequent comment which youth express about the church is of inconsistency on the part of adults. Religious practices and discipline should be an integral part of the home life pattern. Almost all of us can readily identify with the struggles of Keith Miller and his family to initiate family prayer.[8] It rings a bell with any parent who has desired or attempted to do it . . . consistently. The Millers' solution was to do what best "fit" the family, as should every family. Perhaps prayer at the table is right; perhaps father or mother praying with each child before bed. Something must be done, however, and something is "right" for you.

Here, again, even more important than the act is the *interpretation* of it. It is one thing for a child to do, and another to know *why*. All too frequent when I talk with parents over a child rejecting the church in the teen-age years, a deficient pattern of act-without-explanation is present. If I could say anything of spiritual importance to parents, it would be to focus on those value judgments and interpretations beyond the religious activities.

Interpretation plays another vital role in the religious responsibilities of parents: interpreting spiritual crises in the maturing life of a child. A child can make a "decision" for Christ early, but as he grows older the implications of that decision must be reinterpreted to fit his widening perspective. A wise parent aids his child in this deepening and widening spiritual perspective in such a way that his spiritual growth keeps pace with his physical and mental growth.

Both relationships, husband-wife and parent-child, jointly provide a context much needed by all the family members: acceptance and appreciation. This alone is the context in which "becoming" is possible. To accept and appreciate each other as we are allows each to become what he can be. This places a responsibility on each member of the family unit to encourage the other. Warner Baxter, who married Winifred Bryson during her budding stage career, gives us

[8] Keith Miller. *A Second Touch.* (Waco: Word, 1967), pp. 37-48.

the clue to what acceptance and appreciation mean. He said of his wife:

> She missed the applause of stage success, but I have tried to see that she is entirely aware of *my* applause. [9]

HOME AND CHURCH. The third relationship in the framework of a Christ-home is the home and the church. And its first element is that the family share in the same church. If the family is to "keep pace," as mentioned above, this is of cardinal importance.

In marriages which cross denominational lines, a common church *must* be chosen. While any of us can point to happy marriages in which mates have gone to different churches, we can also point to many more which did not work; in those which did accomplish it, we can only wonder "how much more" may have been theirs together. If one or the other's church cannot be chosen, a compromise should be made in a third. If such cannot be done, then both should attend *both!* Every effort must be made to provide a common ground for Christian growth. I am convinced, however, that when two are *obedient* to Christ and honestly seek *His will* in prayer *together*, a solution may be reached. Indeed, if Christ cannot bring two together over something as important and as dear to Him as the Church, we should not expect too much from Him in other areas of needed unity!

In the case of a Christian and a non-Christian, the situation is vastly different. To say that the marriage should not have happened is to ignore a need; it has happened, and answers are needed. Sadly, however, easy answers are lacking. In such a marriage, the Christian member will want to keep his or her faith intact and flourishing as the primary act. Then one can only pray for God's direction and His grace. It is not hopeless, but it is hard. One great value of small groups is that mates are more willing to share in a home venture than in a formal church service.

[9] Quoted in: Dale Carnegie. *How to Win Friends and Influence People.* (New York: Simon & Schuster, 1937), p. 320.

Whatever the course and the circumstances, cultivate a life in which God's leadership can be known. He is there to help.

On the other hand, after church ties have been mutually established, the family should view *the church as the ally of the home*. Don't gloss over this "ally" idea; it is a new one for both home and church today. Most of us work on the premise that we exist to support the church. The better idea is that the church exists to support the home! The church can provide something the home cannot. It provides education in a class of peers, with good literature and teachers. It provides activities which serve as a channel for an outlet of faith. In the church, we support each other and each others' homes as you teach my six-year-old and my wife teaches your ten-year-old. View the church as your ally!

The church must also learn to see itself as the ally of the home — more than it already does. By providing family-wide programs, it allows them to share in an area where sharing is most important: the spiritual life. Thus weeklong studies and conferences should provide classes for all. Family midweek dinners are good, also. More important, however, as a regular part of the church program, are "family life conferences." In these, the focus is entirely on the family and on practicality. Each year, as a part of the Heritage program, we conduct such a conference with a qualified person leading us in a weekend of study together. We also provide a family-oriented retreat over Labor Day weekend, renting a camp and inviting the entire church family. The emphasis is not so much on the family as a topic, but on providing a time and place for the family to be together, away from the pressures of home. After twenty years of retreating, our church family can attest to the value and the blessing of having this kind of opportunity. The church becomes the ally of the home as it provides family-centered programs and opportunities for families to be together.

In the framework of these three relationships — *husband-wife, parent-child,* and *church-home* — we are called upon to minister to others where ministry counts the most. As we seek to demonstrate and spread the kingdom of God, the home is primary territory. Trueblood says:

> It is by the many little kingdoms that the world is changed. These little kingdoms may be of various kinds, but the very best example known to us is the redemptive society which is called a home. [10]

DISCUSSION QUESTIONS

1. Do the group members feel that the family unit is a precise indicator of what is going on in our society? Be specific and explain your answers.

2. What does the term "keeping pace" convey to you in the context of a husband and wife living, growing, talking, and praying together in hopes of building a happy marriage?

3. In what ways can a parent evoke the gifts within a child?

CREATIVE GROUP PROCEDURE

By providing two pipe cleaners to each one, let the group members bend and shape the cleaners to depict (1) the perfect marriage and (2) the perfect home. Each one will then explain why he chose those particular designs. The entire group should complete the first exercise (the perfect marriage) before proceeding to the second.

[10] Elton Trueblood. *The Yoke of Christ.* (New York: Harper & Row, 1958), p. 192.

Chapter Eleven

Bible Study Selection

An angel of the Lord spoke to Philip, "Get yourself ready and go south to the road that goes from Jerusalem to Gaza." (This road is no longer used). So Philip got ready and went. Now an Ethiopian eunuch was on his way home. This man was an important official in charge of the treasury of the Queen, or Candace, of Ethiopia. He had been to Jerusalem to worship God, and was going back in his carriage. As he rode along he was reading from the book of the prophet Isaiah. *The Holy Spirit* said to Philip, "Go over and stay close to that carriage." Philip ran over and heard him reading from the book of the prophet Isaiah; so he asked him, "Do you understand what you are reading?" "How can I understand," the official replied, "unless someone explains it to me?" And he invited Philip to climb up and sit in the carriage with him. . . .

Philip began to speak; starting from this very passage of scripture, he told him the Good News about Jesus. As they traveled down the road they came to a place where there was some water, and the official said, "Here is some water. What is to keep me from being baptized?" Philip said to him, "You may be baptized if you believe with all your heart." "I do," he answered; "I believe that Jesus Christ is the Son of God." The official ordered the carriage to stop; and both of them, Philip and the official, went down into the water, and Philip baptized him.

(Acts 8:26-31, 35-38 TEV, italics added)

CHAPTER ELEVEN

THE LAITY AND EVANGELISM
Wayside or Waylay?

> *The altar might have to become mobile as it was with Israel in the wilderness.*
>
> ADELLE CARLSON

When we read the New Testament with an eye on evangelism (from the Greek word *euaggelion* meaning "good news"), seeking to learn how and what Christ and His early followers did, we make at least three discoveries.

The first is easily anticipated. Evangelism, however one chooses to interpret it, was primary. The emphasis was on "good news-ing" it —

Jesus' teaching to the disciples centered on it;
the term "apostle" means "one sent forth " on a mission;
the training of the Apostles revolved around trial missions;
the Great Commission was emphatic in its evangelistic thrust (Matt. 28:19, 20);
and the last words of Christ in Acts 1:8 are unequivocal — "you shall be witnesses."

The record of the early church in Acts is evidence that they took evangelism as seriously as they did literally. Evangelism was primary.

The second discovery is not always anticipated: Jesus never went out of His way to witness. The great experiences of witness by Christ occurred within the normal course of events: people came to Him or He "bumped into" them as He was passing by. The witness He gave grew out of their natural encounter and exchange. Think of the most memorable of those experiences, and it becomes evident: the woman at the well in Samaria (John 4:1-42), the Gadarene demoniac (Mark 5:1-20), the woman who touched the hem of His garment (Matt. 9:20-22), and the meeting of Zaccheus (Luke 19:1-28). Jesus never had to go out of His way to find opportunity; it was *wayside* witnessing.

Third, the evangelistic ministry of the post-Pentecost followers was Spirit-led witnessing. They looked for and received the guidance of the Holy Spirit as to *when* and *where* and *how*. The miracle of Pentecost and its evangelistic result were in themselves Spirit-prompted and led. Philip was led of the Spirit to the Ethiopian eunuch, whom the Spirit was simultaneously convicting (Acts 8:26-40). Simon was likewise led to Cornelius (Acts 10:1-48). Paul and Barnabas became witnesses because the Spirit said, "Set [them] apart for me for a task" (Acts 13:1-3 *Phillips*). Indeed, the evangelization of Europe was not on Paul's agenda at all! Left to himself, Paul's choice was to go to Bithynia, "but the Spirit of Jesus did not allow them" (Acts 16:7); the Spirit's choice was Europe, via Troas and Philippi. New Testament evangelism is always Spirit-led witnessing.

As we think of the lay ministry today, then, and the incumbent responsibility to spread the Kingdom, these three discoveries become significant to us.

On the other hand, when the contemporary Church is viewed with an eye on evangelism, the difference is rather bold in contrast with the New Testament. Immediately noticeable is that our evangelism is largely *mass-centered rather than personal.* Our evangelistic mainstays are crusades, revivals, Sunday school, youth rallies, and now bus ministries. Our "reports" focus on the *numbers;* the New Testament focused on *names* — individual persons. Indeed, most of our evangelistic tools are impersonal: tracts, radio, television, bumper stickers, and lapel buttons.

The other prominent difference is that contemporary evangelism is *highly programed*. Crusade planning is now a highly polished art. Even local church evangelism is — the census, the survey, Thursday night visitation, and report cards with spaces for five different visitors to report the "results." Visitation techniques are widely taught — "approaches," we call them: what to say, when to say it, what to do when they accept or reject, and what to leave in their hands for "follow up" — all *programed*.

This is not to say contemporary evangelism is wrong; it is merely noting that it is different. In truth, the ministry of "evangelism" is one gift of the Spirit (Eph. 4:11), and the ministries of many modern evangelists obviously bear the mark of God. Without crusades, revivals, and these modern programs, we would be without any tools. But these differences have some observable disadvantages. The emphasis on numbers works against the focus on the personal — inevitably. Persons become "prospects" or "decisions," but as Baron Von Hugel reminded us, "souls are never dittoes." The highly programed approach works against the leadership of the Holy Spirit, and we are not always as careful as we ought to be about compensating for it. Dr. Carl Bates, past president of the Southern Baptist Convention, says, "If God called His Holy Spirit out of the world, about 95 percent of what we are doing would go on and we would brag about it!"

One element of modern evangelism, however, deserves more than the "different" label; *it is wrong*. That is, there is a strand of contemporary evangelism built on the premise of what can only be called "tricky salesmanship." There are "right" questions to ask to evoke the "right" answers. There are "right" sized testaments to carry, testaments which are to be "hidden" in pocket or purse until the "right" time. The emphasis is to get them to accept a *plan*, and it is not always made clear that salvation means to accept a *Person*, not a *plan*. We "nail it down" and often get "decisions," but there can be a difference between decisions and disciples. Jesus did not view salvation as a one-time experience like a spiritual vaccination; He called for followers, not admirers. Usually this onesided emphasis is on "Savior" rather than "Lord" — if one can in fact separate them. And if this approach does not work, there is always the "I'm taking a survey of religious attitudes — could I ask you a few questions?" technique. The final question gives you an opportunity to engage them in the "three steps" or the "six principles" or whatever.

This is not to say that those who use this means are dishonest. Never! They are frequently the most concerned persons Christ has! Nor is it to say there is no plan of salvation. But it is to say that this approach is built on a premise of tricky salesmanship — it is exactly the same way you sell Sput-a-matic sweepers or A-tom products! In many ways, it is more akin to the word *waylay* than it is to *wayside* evangelism! (Once, as we were preparing to teach a course in personal evangelism, a layman suggested to me that we should not teach it publicly since some unsaved person might hear us and know what we are up to when we witness to him!) The frightening implication of it all is that there is apparently a fear on the part of some that the Gospel cannot or will not be accepted on its own merits; that people have to be "tricked" into it; that our task is to *waylay* them "for Jesus." When we contrast such methods with Jesus' — His open, transparent, honest, forthright manner — the word "Christlike" all but drops to a whisper.

The question arises, "If this is not the way, what is it?" And it is a proper question. The trouble with mass evangelism is not that it is wrong, for it is a gift. The trouble is that mass evangelism has become a *replacement for* instead of a *supplement to* the "wayside witnessing" which is the primary emphasis of the New Testament. It suggests that only a few are to do what *all* are supposed to be doing. The trouble with our personal evangelism is that, while the premise of some of it is wrong, it is the only kind being done. Wayside witnessing is an *unemployed* option. The

real truth is that what is *everyone's* business — witnessing —
is almost *no one's* business today.

WAYSIDE WITNESSING. What, then, does "wayside witnessing" involve? Perhaps some basic definitions are needed
first. Of the two, *evangelism* and *witnessing*, evangelism is
the more difficult to define — and upon which to achieve
unanimity. There is more agreement, however, than we
often are led to believe. Two definitions from vastly different backgrounds illustrate this: one from the World Congress on Evangelism held in West Berlin in 1966, sponsored
by *Christianity Today* and chaired by Billy Graham, and
the other from the Church of England, "The Archbishop's
Committee of Inquiry on the Evangelistic Work of the
Church," in 1918.

Church of England	*World Congress*
"To evangelize is so to present Christ Jesus in the power of the Holy Spirit that men shall come to put their trust in God through Him, to accept Him as their Savior, and serve Him as their King in the fellowship of His Church." [1]	"Evangelism is the proclamation of the Gospel of the crucified and risen Christ, the only Redeemer of men, according to the Scriptures, with the purpose of persuading condemned and lost sinners to put their trust in God by receiving and accepting Christ as Savior through the power of the Holy Spirit, and to serve Christ as Lord in every calling of life and in the fellowship of His Church, looking toward the day of His coming in glory." [2]

Frederick Speakman says we have fallen victim to "Little
Bo-Beep's Mistake"; that the lost sheep will come home on

[1] Quoted in: Charles S. Duthie. *God in His World* (Nashville: Abingdon), pp. 128-29.
[2] Carl F. H. Henry. *Evangelicals on the Brink of Crisis*. (Waco: Word,
1967), p. 37.

their own initiative![3] Carl Henry gives an accurate assessment:

> We sing "like a mighty army moves the Church of God," but an army that captures only one or two stragglers a year is hardly worth the name.[4]

"Witnessing," on the other hand, is a *mode* or *method* of evangelism. Strictly speaking, it refers to a personal report of the work of Christ in one's life. It is to say with John, "that . . . which we have seen with our [own] eyes . . . we proclaim also to you" (1 John 1:1-3). Urie A. Bender, in one of the most wholesome books on the subject of witnessing in print, says:

> One witnesses when he gives evidence based on knowledge gained from experience. In the Christian context one witnesses when he shares his knowledge of God's grace based on his own experiences of faith in Christ. . . .
> To witness is to share. Haltingly, perhaps. Without polish, usually. Out of experience, always.[5]

This "witness" will include one's life prior to accepting Christ, the context and factors of the decision, and a statement of pilgrimage todate. It will, of course, use Scripture, the testimonial witness of others, and illustrations; but these are used as allies and supplements to the personal report. Witnessing is always first person singular — *my* report of Christ's activity in *my* life.[6]

> Wayside witnessing is sharing your "interim report" with others whom you meet in the normal flow of daily activities as the Holy Spirit leads you.

Witnessing involves five basic elements. First, it is . . .

Universal. When C. E. Matthews was asked to write a book on "personal evangelism" for his denomination, he de-

[3] Frederick Speakman. *God and Jack Wilson.* (Westwood, N. J.: Revell, 1965), p. 99.

[4] Henry. *The God Who Shows Himself,* p. 102.

[5] From *The Witness* by Urie A. Bender. Copyright © 1965 by Herald Press, Scottdale, PA 15683. Used by permission.

[6] See: Neighbour, *The Touch of the Spirit,* chapter 9. This book is subtitled: "A Spirit-filled Approach to Witnessing."

liberately and accurately chose the title, *Every Christian's Job.* [7] It is just that: *every* follower's task. Teaching a class, being an usher, singing in the choir, paying tithes — all are good and needed, but they may not be *substituted* for witnessing; no one can either "buy off" or "beg off." As Trueblood says, "The non-witnessing Christian is a contradiction in terms." Wayside witnessing for the lay minister begins with this universal emphasis. Second, it is . . .

Natural. Wayside witnessing is done "as you go." Jesus said to His disciples, "And preach *as you go*" (Matt. 10:7, italics added). This is also the literal meaning of the Great Commission in Matthew 28:19, 20: not "go ye," but "*as you go.*" Witnessing is not "go and do," but "do as you go." It is done within the framework of your normal daily schedule. How often we misread Jesus' familiar call, "Follow me and I will make you fishers of men." We think He said, "Go and I will make you . . ."; but *He* said, "Follow me — and I will *make* you fishers . . ." as you *follow along!* As with Christ, Christ-*ians* do not have to go out of their way to witness! Third, it is . . .

Spirit-led. Perhaps the greatest difference between witnessing as-it-is and witnessing as-it-should-be is the place of the Holy Spirit in it. The New Testament gives two definite assurances about the ministry of the Spirit. One is that the Holy Spirit is always at work in the world convicting men of their need of God. Jesus was emphatic in saying that "when He comes, he *will* convince (literally "convince and keep on convincing") the world . . ." (John 16:8, italics added.) The second assurance is that the Spirit will lead Christians at all times; indeed, "as many as are led by the Spirit of God, these are the sons of God" (Rom. 8:14 KJV).

When applied to witnessing, this means the Holy Spirit who is *convicting* one person is also *leading* another person, a Christian, — *to bring them together!* The examples of Philip with the Ethiopian eunuch and Peter with Cornelius

---

[7] C. E. Matthews. *Every Christian's Job.* (Nashville: Convention Press, 1951).

are typical of the New Testament style of witnessing. All too frequently we stifle this requirement of sensitivity to the Spirit's leadership *in the instant* for a spontaneous, natural witness by . . . *giving out cards!* "Go visit this family," we say. "They are 'prospects.'" (Many times, they are barely "suspects"!) Though the Spirit works within this haphazard system (it is all He has with which to work!), our batting average ought to tell us something. The only surefire method is to trust the One who *alone* knows who is "ready" for a witness. Urie A. Bender says:

> Actually, the Spirit works at two points. Through circumstances of many kinds He prepares a heart step by step. Then He seeks to direct, at the opportune moment, a witness of God's grace to the heart thus prepared. To run ahead of the Spirit can be as devastating as to refuse to follow. [8]

Fourth, wayside witnessing is . . .

Personal. By "personal" is meant several things. It means *one-to-one* witnessing. It also means that the person being sought is a *person,* not just a soul. He has a *name* as well as a *need.*

Likewise, the object of our witnessing is as important as the subject. Why are we trying to win the person? It is said that when William Booth of the Salvation Army received reports of no moves, he always replied "Thy tears!" But *why* tears? Christ's concern was *what they were missing,* how they were *short-changing* themselves! And it broke His heart. Thus His favorite synonym for salvation was "to be made whole." To seek to "win" others to get new members, to reach a quota, to strike or keep an average, or to win a free trip to the Holy Land — is to *prostitute* the Gospel. It leads to "scalp-hunting" ("look how many I got tonight!") and to a "souls-only" approach which makes persons mere "notches on a Gospel gun." Valid witnessing is always personal, one-to-one, and person-centered. Last, wayside witnessing is . . .

[8] Urie Bender. *Op. cit.,* p. 146.

Cultivative. Cultivative witnessing recognizes that people are not usually, if ever, won overnight. We are sometimes misled by the gospel accounts which seem to imply that Jesus arrived on the scene and said "Follow me" to complete strangers, and they did. What we fail to see is that these accounts are abbreviated reports. This cultivation requirement can be illustrated with Nicodemus. His first encounter with Christ is in John 3. Obviously, but unreported, he had heard Christ speak (or others speak about Him) to the degree that he sought Him out. But Jesus pressed home no decision. It was one of those "think about it" encounters. The next reference to Nicodemus comes some two years later when he defended Jesus in a private session with his fellow Pharisees (John 7:50, 51). Clearly, Nicodemus was not yet a follower; he had only moved from "seeker" to "sympathizer." The next reference is much later, nearly a year, when he openly joined Joseph in claiming the body of Jesus for burial (John 19:39, 40). *A three-year period of cultivation!*

This kind of evangelism recognizes that much witnessing is seed-sowing rather than harvesting, and that many witnesses may share in the cultivative process. Because of this and because many times we recognize that another Christian is better equipped or has more in common with the person, we put them in contact with each other as the Spirit leads us. Thus we become instruments of the Holy Spirit in the processes of both cultivation and harvest.

Wayside witnessing, therefore, is done (1) in the normal flow of life (2) as the Spirit leads us (3) by sharing our "interim report" of Christ's activity in our lives. The idea is to go "good news-ing" it, ever sensitive to our ever-present Guide, the Holy Spirit.

For the concerned layman this means witnessing may take on an entirely new perspective! No longer need it be a planned speech on a scheduled night to a complete stranger. More people are passing through our lives in the daily course of living that we could ever meet through a survey! It means we can engage each new day with the absolute assurance that God the Holy Spirit is already up and at work — with others and with us — and when the "moment of truth" comes, He will bring us together. It is His *assignment* — and our *promise!* We can go in excited anticipation of it.

But will it work and will it work better than what we are presently doing? The only honest answer is — no one really knows. *We haven't tried it!* To be sure, the numerical statistics of present methods are not to be discounted, but it depends upon when they are counted, too: the same night or five years later? Whatever else one may say about mass evangelism, he *must* say that the attrition rate is extremely high. Jesus called us to bear fruit, but He also desired that our fruit remain (John 15:16). About all we have left many times are the *scalps* — but no *bodies!* Far too many of our "converts" seem to be on "one-year contracts" (or less) with Christ. But if Christ is our pattern and if the Spirit's two-fold ministry is still in operation, the answer is clear: yes, it will work! I agree with Dr. José Martinez of Barcelona, Spain, who said at the World Congress on Evangelism:

> Christians filled with the Holy Spirit will always find an effective way to evangelize. But the best systems will fail if the power of the Holy Spirit is lacking. [9]

DISCUSSION QUESTIONS

1. Recalling that Jesus did not go out of His way to witness, but His witness occurred in the natural flow of events, have the group discuss the dominant trends of evangelism today.

2. Allow each group member to assess his responsibility in Spirit-led evangelism. Think in terms of the *preparation* required for a person to be sensitive to His leadership.

3. By allowing each to employ his own choice of words, let the group members define "witness" and "evangelism."

[9] Quoted in: Henry. *Evangelicals on the Brink of Crisis,* p. 46.

CREATIVE GROUP PROCEDURE

An innovative approach to this session is to view the film, "The Gospel Blimp," and discuss it together. (Sacred Cinema, 40 min., $25).

Or, let each person devise a "church program" of *personal* evangelism, suggesting training procedures, inner life disciplines necessary to it, and specific target groups to evangelize. Be personal, developing the program for your situation.

Or, see the author's *Renew My Church* (p. 62) and discuss the use of "plans of salvation."

Or, see Ralph Neighbour's *The Touch of the Spirit* (pp. 106-108) and complete the study noted there of Christ's conversation with the Samaritan woman. This should be mimeographed or duplicated in advance.

Chapter Twelve

Bible Study Selection

So, by virtue of the blood of Jesus, you and I, my brothers, may now have confidence to enter the Holy of Holies by a fresh and living way, which he has opened up for us by himself passing through the curtain, that is, his own human nature. Further, since we have a great High Priest set over the household of God, let us draw near with true hearts and fullest confidence, knowing that our inmost souls have been purified by the sprinkling of his blood just as our bodies are cleansed by the washing of clean water.

In this confidence let us hold on to the hope that we profess without the slightest hesitation — for he is utterly dependable — and let us think of one another and how we can *encourage each other* to love and do good deeds. And let us not hold aloof from our church meetings, as some do. Let us do all we can to *help one another's faith,* and this the more earnestly as we see the final day drawing ever nearer.

(Heb. 10:19-25 *Phillips,* italics added)

CHAPTER TWELVE

THE LAITY AND ENCOURAGEMENT
Lifter or Leaner?

> *Never morning wore*
> *To evening, but some*
> *heart did break.*
> TENNYSON

That there is a need for mutual encouragement, both in the world and in the churches, is not a foregone conclusion today. Perhaps it never was. But it is true that we are not always aware that there is such a thing as . . .

THE NEED FOR ENCOURAGEMENT.   One author recently related an unforgettable childhood experience. As a boy growing up in Florida, he earned money in the fall of the year by raking leaves after school. The seven-year-old daughter of one family delighted in following him about, playfully rescattering the leaves as he worked one day. Urging her several times to stop, to no avail, he finally warned her he would have to tell her father. The author reports:

> She stopped, looked at me in anger, took a straight pin out of her pinafore, ran up to me and stuck me with the pin on the back of my hand. I pulled back my hand and exclaimed, "Ouch! Have you lost your mind?" Whereupon she said in utter astonishment, "That did not hurt you — *you can't feel.*" [1]

[1] Howard Thurman. *The Luminous Darkness.* (New York: Harper & Row, 1965), p. 7, italics added.

You see, Howard Thurman is black.

Sometimes we think some others have no feelings and do not hurt as the rest of us do: prostitutes, homosexuals, divorcees, alcoholics, derelicts, bartenders, ex-convicts, addicts, hippies. Sometimes we even forget that "good" people can do hurt. Many a faithful follower has fallen because there was no one to lift him with a word or a hand.

Our mass-produced, IBM-catalogued, anonymous society has only intensified the personal need for fellowship, warmth, love, and encouragement. Used as we are and manipulated, Charles Reich flatly charges: "America is one vast anti-community." [2] We live in what one has labeled "overcrowded isolation." Yes, the need is there.

The Church is often a part of the problem rather than the solution, both toward the world and toward each other. Bishop Gerald Kennedy relates that one of his student pastorates had air conditioning and advertised on the outdoor bulletin board: "Cool inside." Someone chalked on the sign the confirmation, "You said it, brother!" [3] Almost everyone *involved* in the church today knows the reality of the need — *personally*, if no other way. Yet we often fail "to do unto others as we would have others do unto us." (Remember *that* saying?)

The late W. E. Sangster told of a minister who was away from home fulfilling an engagement. Late in the evening he decided to telephone his wife, and as he waited for the operator to complete the call, he hummed and sang a favorite hymn. Suddenly, from somewhere across the land came a startling voice: "Sing it again! Sing it again!" When he did, the voice simply and softly said, "Thank you. Thank you." Who was it? Who knows? But the question could probably be more easily answered by asking, "Who wasn't it?"

It could very well be that the Church has no greater calling in our time than . . . *encouragement*. That we should

[2] Charles Reich. *The Greening of America*. (New York: Random House, 1971), p. 7.

[3] Gerald Kennedy. *For Laymen and Other Martyrs*. (New York: Harper & Row, 1969), p. 29.

fail to see it and do it would be a tragic irony in light of
the biblical examples given us. It is both a scriptural motif
and a Christian mandate. Think of David and Jonathan
when David was fleeing from Saul, fearful in heart and
troubled in mind. God had called him, but why this?

> David well knew that Saul had come out to seek his life,
> and while he was at Horesh . . . Jonathan came to him
> there and gave him fresh courage in God's name.
>   (1 Sam. 23:15, 16 NEB)

One of Paul's loneliest moments must have been as he
trudged up the road to Rome to be imprisoned and tried —
for doing God's will. Surely his mind was reeling and his
heart staggering at the paradox of it all. Luke, however,
records that when the brothers at Rome heard of Paul's
coming, they came out to meet him and "on seeing them
Paul thanked God and took courage" (Acts 28:15).

Isaiah foresaw the kingdom of God. One of its chief char-
acteristics was:

> Every one helps his neighbor, and says to his brother,
> "Take courage!" The craftsman encourages the gold-
> smith, and he who smooths with the hammer him who
> strikes the anvil, saying of the soldering, "It is good."
>   (Isa. 41:6, 7)

If the church is the local branch office of the kingdom,
then we are called to demonstrate this kingdom characteristic *now*. The transition from *ekklesia* (the assembly) to
koinonia (the fellowship) is difficult, but it is ours to make
in the power of the Spirit. "The true difference between
a crowd and a fellowship," says John Oman, "is that in the
former we help to sweep each other off our feet and that
in the latter it is our supreme task to help one another find
our own feet." [4] What we must see clearly is that encouragement will not come from things; it will come from *persons*,
and *only* persons — you and me! But far too many of us are
more like Job's friends than Paul's. My friend Jess Moody
is both quick and apt in his reminder: "We are not here to

---

[4] Quoted in: Charles S. Duthie. *God In His World*, p. 58.

see through each other but to *see each other through!"* In
our better moments, we know it, of course. We just fail
to do it. And our constant failure to be aware of the need
indicates a spiritual shortsightedness; indeed, a spiritual in-
sensitivity. Elton Trueblood says:

> A man has made a step toward a genuine maturity
> when he realizes that, though he ought to perform kind
> and just acts, the greatest gift he can provide others
> consists in being a radiant and encouraging person. [5]

In all of our "doing" for Christ, we must *do* encouragement by *being* encouraging. How? First, we must be clear
about . . .

THE NATURE OF ENCOURAGEMENT. The first step toward
encouragement as a ministry is not a *doing* step, but a
being one. That is, it takes a certain kind of person to be
an "Encourager." He must first be *encouraged* himself, or
all that he says and does is recognizably counterfeit. An
encouraging person must radiate Christian confidence, a
confidence born of a tested faith which bears witness to
Christ's constant ability to do more than we can ask or
think. Christian confidence is that which *knows* that God
is never at a loss as to what to do next.

The encourager's confidence is likewise blended with *joy,*
and joy is one of the exclusive "fruits of the Spirit." Joy,
like the other fruits which Paul lists in Galatians 5:22, 23, is
far more than an ornament on the tree — which it is for far
too many of us; it is a *produced fruit.* Thus, the encourager
is first of all one with deep inner resources, an attribute resulting from a constant inner walk with Christ. The one who
would outwardly encourage others must inwardly cultivate
his own spirit. Naturalness in encouraging will then begin
to *stem* from within, and "stem" is an exact term.

Authentic encouragement will also begin to spring from
us as we begin to feel others' needs and to pray for them.
One encourager I know daily prays for two families in his
congregation by keeping his church directory with his de-

[5] Trueblood. *New Man for Our Time,* p. 79.

votional books; and encouragement seems automatic with him. Sharing-groups discover that it is easier to encourage one another when they first pray for them. First, then, the encourager must begin with himself. Having started with the "first person singular," he forever omits the second person "you" and the third person "they"; he is exclusively a plural "we" person. And, a "we" person discovers ways of being everyman's ally.

Second, the encourager knows his objective. To "encourage" another is to enable him to keep on doing right, to face reality but expect miracles, to be bold and confident *because of Christ.* He shows concern, he exercises care, but above all, he emits confidence in Christ. He knows and shares that real "reality" must include God within the data of experience.

Listening. The title itself of John Drakeford's book, *The Awesome Power of the Listening Ear,* is an incitement to listening, and anyone would do well to read it. [6] Douglas Steere's, *On Listening to Another,* is also a valuable aid. [7] The encourager is always one with his antennae up. He listens for clues which indicate needs. His gift is to read between the lines and hear the under- and overtones of those with whom he speaks. He knows how, as one has stated it, "to reach tenderly into the soul and feel along the rim of the heart for the inevitable crack."

On the other hand, when he is called upon to listen, he does just that — and consequently says more encouragement than words could ever convey. The existence of "hot lines" in our time, with faceless persons who listen on the other end of a telephone to nameless voices, is enough evidence to verify the need. One voice said:

> Listen to me for a day — an hour! — a moment! lest I
> expire in my terrible wilderness, my lonely silence!
> O God, is there no one to listen? [8]

[6] John Drakeford. *The Awesome Power of the Listening Ear.* (Waco: Word, 1967).

[7] This is a two-volume book under one cover along with Steere's *On Beginning From Within.* (New York: Harper & Row, 1964).

[8] Drakeford. *The Awesome Power of the Listening Ear,* p. 81.

That was Seneca, the Roman poet. Just before he committed suicide! How many others are saying it . . . and thinking the other, too? *Listen!*

Watching. While Jesus told us to keep our eyes on the harvest fields, He could have very well said to keep them also on the . . . *harvesters.* Those who are laborers in the fields are those most often in need of encouragement. We must cultivate the habit of watching — watching *for* and *out* for them. A great many of our compatriots are doing different tasks, monotonous ministries and, some of them, impossible ones. One of the most memorable prayers in my life was a brief, one-sentence prayer which simply said, "Lord, it's tough out there." Dr. George W. Truett used to tell of a fireman rescuing a person from a burning building. Carrying the unconscious victim down the ladder, the fireman was suddenly engulfed and overcome by smoke. As the fireman staggered under the load momentarily, the fire chief below shouted to the others on the ground: "Cheer him! Cheer him!" It gave the fireman the boost of courage he needed to finish the job.

Not only do actively engaged persons need encouragement, the passive failures do, also! All of us don't always "make it" all the time. *We fail.* The encourager learns to see a failing brother in just that way: *we* fail. Jeremiah's experience at the house of the potter (Jer. 18:1-11), when the marred vessel was remade, means even more to us when we accept the truth that we are the hands of God used in remolding scarred lives. Barnabas is without peer as example of failure redemption. John Mark, who fled the cause on Paul's first missionary journey (Acts 13:13), would have been lost to the Church had it not been for Barnabas. So adament was Paul's refusal to try to reclaim Mark for the next journey that it prompted a split between Paul and Barnabas (Acts 15:36-40). Barnabas, however, took Mark with him on his mission and one of the most meaningful passages in all the New Testament is when Paul, nearly thirty years later on the eve of his death, wrote to Timothy:

"Get Mark and bring him with you; for he is very useful in serving me" (2 Tim. 4:11).

Grouping.   Among all its other assets, the small group has done as much encouraging as anything in the kingdom's cause. Designed to strengthen each other, to sharpen one another's swords, encouragement is a natural by-product of groups. If it is true, to paraphrase Francis Bacon, that "friendship doubles joy and halves sorrow," think what multiplication and division a caring *group* can do!

Writing.   The power to encourage through letters, notes, and cards is often overlooked, yet it is one of immeasurable impact. While it perhaps reveals a flaw in us, most of us can express things of an intimate, caring nature better in writing than in other ways. Elton Trueblood has a "government postcard" ministry — with an uncanny ability to know just when they are needed. Not long ago, a pastor friend suffered a blow when one of his "Timothy's" became a "Demas," and I dropped him a quick note of encouragement. His immediate response by mail showed the value of it. Thoughts like "I was thinking of you," "praying for," "grateful for" are often all that is needed to keep another on his feet and in the fight.

Being.   Strength to the weak hands, feeble knees, and fearful hearts, as Isaiah expressed it (Isa. 35:3, 4), is more "imparted" than given or spoken . . . just by *being there.* While it bears a modern label — "non-verbal communication," all of us have known it and received it. It comes from a smile, a pat on the back, an arm around the shoulder, or simply a glance from readable eyes. Our word "comfort" comes from the Latin *con-fortis,* meaning "strong together." Very often we can draw on the strength of speechless companions whose presence alone says all. The evidence of this periodic need is seen in nothing less than the life of Jesus. The night before His death, as the Twelve-minus-one entered the Garden, He asked Peter, James, and John to go on further with Him — just to "watch" while He prayed. Silent, caring presence is often the only encouragement we can give, and many times the best.

One of the great values of the book of Hebrews, and one often overlooked, is its intent to encourage. Obviously written in a time of persecution, discouragement, and fear, when the threat and temptation to desert was an ever-present, haunting option, Hebrew's theme is: "Hold fast!"

> But Christ was faithful over God's house as a son. And we are his house if we hold fast our confidence and pride in our hope.   (Heb. 3:6)

> For we share in Christ, if only we hold our first confidence firm to the end.   (Heb. 3:14)

> Since then we have a great high priest who has passed through the heavens, Jesus, the Son of God, let us hold fast our confession.   (Heb. 4:14)

> Let us hold fast the confession of our hope without wavering, for he who promised is faithful; and let us consider how to stir up one another to love and good works, not neglecting to meet together, as is the habit of some, but encouraging one another, and all the more as you see the Day drawing near.   (Heb. 10:23-25)

And the long listing of the faithful saints and their problems in Chapter Eleven is but to say:

> Therefore, since we are surrounded by so great a cloud of witnesses, let us also lay aside every weight, and sin which clings so closely, and let us run with perseverance the race that is set before us.   (Heb. 12:1)

"In times like these" most of us do need an *anchor*. More often, however, we need help with the *hoisting of our sails* — to catch the wind of the Spirit in the service of Christ. Encouragement is nothing less than a *ministry* today!

Perhaps, in the end, it is true that:

> There are two kinds of people on earth today,
> Just two kinds of people, no more, I say,
> Not the good and the bad, for 'tis well understood
> The good are half bad and the bad are half good.

Not the happy and sad, for the swift flying years
Bring each man his laughter and each man his tears.
Not the rich and the poor, for to count a man's wealth
You must first know the state of his conscience and health.

Not the humble and proud, for in life's busy span
Who puts on vain airs is not counted a man.
No! The two kinds of people on earth I mean
Are the people who lift, and the people who lean.

ELLA WHEELER WILCOX

DISCUSSION QUESTIONS

1. From the experience of the group, discuss what value "encouragement" has been in your life in specific incidents.

2. Discuss the concept of "The Need for Encouragement." Several group members convey to the group a time in their lives when a little encouragement would have meant much, but never came.

3. In light of this chapter the group might discuss encouragement as a ministry for each one.

CREATIVE GROUP PROCEDURE

Let the group role play a group session on *encouragement* by assigning various members certain roles. Let each character come before the group with a "discouragement." The group should then discuss how to go about encouraging this person during the next week or so. Possible characters: a pastor who seems to be getting no response from his people as he preaches on a deeper walk with Christ; a mother whose single daughter is away at college and living with a male student; a black man, thirty-five years old, who has been denied a promotion in an evident case of discrimination; a husband whose wife just left him for another man; a group member who just confessed she is an alcoholic. The group may select other characters, avoiding any embarrassment to group members.

PART THREE

Chapter Thirteen

Bible Study Selection

So be sure you do not refuse to hear the voice of God! For if they who refuse to hear those who spoke to them on earth did not escape, how little chance of escape is there for us if we refuse to hear the one who speaks from Heaven. Then his voice shook the earth, but now he promises:

> Yet once more will I make to tremble
> Not the earth only, but also the heaven.

This means that in this final "shaking" all that is impermanent will be removed, that is, everything that is merely "made," and *only the unshakable things will remain.*

Since then we have been given a kingdom that is "unshakable," let us serve God with thankfulness in the *ways which please Him,* but always with reverence and holy fear. For it is perfectly true that our God is a burning fire.

(Heb. 12:25-29 *Phillips*, italics added)

THE LAITY AND THE FUTURE

Vanguard or Rearguard?

*The man who is wedded
to his time will soon be
a widower.*

ELTON TRUEBLOOD

[My original intention was to make this final chapter an "epilogue" on the future of the organized church. There were so many ideas struggling to be born and included in *The Idea of the Laity* which, because they were unsteady on their new legs, could not merit the label of "I can faithfully report to you"; they were only "I have a feeling" ideas. Wilmer Cooper, dean of the Earlham School of Religion, taught me always to play the "holy hunches," but these are still only diagrams on the chalkboard in the locker room.

The more I have toyed with them, however, the more I have wanted to share them. My batting average indicates that some of them are doubtlessly bad guesses, but, with the hope that there might be a "holy hunch" or two among them, I share them for our mutual refinement.

Since it is really more a "catalogue" than an "epilogue," the only possible order to follow is . . . alphabetical!]

ANACHRONISM. A good example of what is meant by "anachronism" has to do with those buttons on men's coat sleeves: still being used after their purpose has been forgotten. Originally those buttons were used to attach ruffles to the sleeves! Like the old celluloid collar, sleeve ruffles were not permanent attachments to shirts; they were additives. The Church has its buttons, too! They are programs, organizations, methods, and styles — still being employed long after their purposes are forgotten and their functions outlived. While this is not true of all the Church's program paraphernalia, it is true of some. A continuing problem for the Church is that once a method is adopted, it becomes a permanent attachment. Consequently, the Church is continually slowed in its advance because it must drag along so much excess baggage. We must teach our people the difference between a permanent attachment and an additive which can go out of style. Have you looked at your church's coat sleeves lately?

CONVERSION. More and more I am convinced the biggest hindrance to renewal is that many in need of *re-newal* have never been made *new* in the first place. There must be a conversion in the life of a Christian. It is true that we have added many things to the initial experience of the Christ-life, things like weeping, "going forward," coming to the altar, giving up habits, etc., etc., none of which are of the Truth. But all of this does not for a moment abrogate the absolute necessity of conversion. As Bruce Larson says, this "means that at some point in time we have by an act of the will turned the management of our lives over to Jesus Christ." [1] That is, there is a time and a place where we, in prayer, begin our walk with Christ. We may not remember the date and hour, but we know that it happened.

How does it come about, however? "By an act of the will," Larson says. Dr. James Mahoney, who is without peer today in presenting the "deeper life" concept, once asked

[1] Bruce Larson. *Setting Men Free.* (Grand Rapids: Zondervan, 1967), pp. 22-23.

me, "Where is a person saved?" My answer was, "In the will, in the volitional center of his being." This is true because becoming a Christian entails turning "the management of our lives over to Jesus Christ," and this is the business of the will.

One of the most active members of our Yokefellow One group was a young man who, after companying and serving with the group for some months, realized he was trying to *be* a Christian when he had never *become* one. He made his commitment — the management of his life — in the presence of the entire group on a retreat, and now is not only *active*, he is *effective*. And, that is the difference conversion makes.

COSMOPOLITAN CHURCHES.   Nearly every church in the urban, cosmopolitan areas of our nation is faced with the problem of programing to suit diversified needs and wants. As people migrate to a new area from many other areas and identify with a local church, they invariably bring both a *form* and a *faith* with them. (Sometimes, I think, more of the former than the latter!) Different ways, different times, different styles, and different titles — and each wants a little bit of home in every church. Usually the "established" group *resents* the new group, and the new group *pities* the old group. Consequently there is a great need for pastors to interpret to the people what is going on *sociologically* and to guide them into *actualizing the kingdom idea:* unity exists because of our common Lord and labor, not by program structures and terminology.

DENOMINATIONS.   Most current denominations built their program structure about one hundred years ago. That is, most of our present boards, agencies, commissions, districts, and associations, were in existence then. Change has come, of course, but most of it has been *within* the structures, not in *new* structures. This does not mean they *ipso facto* need to be changed, but it does indicate something: if they were designed a hundred years ago, they were designed for a homogeneous society. Nearly all our denominationally sponsored clinics and symposia are still being conducted on some form of regional basis. While this could once be done, and in some areas can still be done, it is increasingly more impossible to find similar churches with similar needs even across town! One change on the denominational agenda must be that the staff members who relate to the church programs of education, training, and missions become *local church consultants* rather than regional representatives. The tailor-made local church program is the thing of the future; churches will need help in programing for *their* needs.

DIVISION.   Division in the Church is often misunderstood. That is, many believe denominationalism represents a divided Church when, in truth, it does not. The different emphases and styles of various groups would be lost without denominations. Unity exists apart from union. Doctrine divides some of us, but close examination invariably reveals we are more alike than different. What, then, is the really *divisive* element? I do not know about today, but tomorrow's challenge to our unity will be *methodological;* it will have to do with structural innovation within churches and denominations. Somehow we must learn the age-old adage that there is more than one way to skin a cat . . . and to operate a church. Someone has said we are "too soft to split," and that may be true doctrinally. But structural change breeds just the opposite result: *rigidity* of methods and styles will be *the* problem tomorrow.

The answer to it? Unity is solely the result of the Holy Spirit controlling all of us. Our work is not so much to force cooperation with each other as it is to willingly cooperate with Him.

ECUMENISM.   As a movement toward union, ecumenism is dead. The trend now is to recognize that unity does not necessarily require union, as stated above. We stand to lose far more than we gain by diluting the various denominational emphases, which would occur in union. There is, however, another emerging ecumenical trend, a negative one. It is a growing and obvious lack of denominational loyalty among the younger generation. There was a time when a Baptist or a Methodist moved to a new community that he took membership in the local denominational church . . . regardless. But no more! People are looking for local churches which meet their needs, not for denominational labels. In many ways this is a healthy trend, for it indicates people are making deliberate, personal choices rather than automatic ones; it implies that they "mean business" far more than before. The one big danger in this, however, is the absence of any loyalty to denominations. The greater part of the Church's ministries in hospitals, orphanages, foreign missions, and inner city work is done on a denominational basis with denominational funding. All of this could collapse — and local congregations cannot carry it on due to the costs involved — if denominational loyalty totally collapses. We must encourage the healthy trends while warning of the dangers.

EVANGELISM. We are seeing an almost unprecedented sociological phenomenon today in group patterns which will affect our evangelistic methods. Always before the trend has been toward assimilation and integration when migration occurs. The European groups which came to America lived in ghetto fashion for a while, but assimilation into the greater community always followed. Now, however, the trend is reversing! Groups are now regrouping. The reason for it is largely the quest for identity. There is little to lend itself to individuality in our computer-card society, and now ethnic and racial groups are regrouping for personal and individual identity via the group. They are resurrecting speech and dress patterns and in some cases even inventing them.

Another affecting factor is that the housing trend of the future is rental. Right now more than half of the housing being built in America is rental. And the trend within housing is toward specific groups: singles housing and retirement centers, for example. But, aside from the reasons for it, the implications of it are important to our future evangelistic programs. Isn't this going to require a specialized, "target-group" strategy rather than our present general approach?

FLEXIBILITY. Societal change in the past has followed a discernible pattern of plateaus: an advance was made and a relatively stable plateau followed. The rapidity of change today has abbreviated the plateau stage; the reduction of it to constant flux is fast nearing us. Organizational structures, designed to meet needs, have a built-in time lag, however. It simply requires time for the change to be felt, grasped, and to filter down to the grass roots. (The time lag in medicine is now approximately ten years from the research lab to the local G.P.). Denominational, organizational, and local congregational structures will be affected by this, and the answer to our present *bureaucracy* is what Alvin Toffler calls *ad-hocracy:* a built-in flexibility to adapt and attack new problems immediately. [2] The sometime competitive nature of many church organizations is a luxury the future will not afford us!

FUTURE. Any lover of the Church and the churches must be concerned with its future, the only future which cannot and must not anticipate retirement. To be wedded to today is to be a widower tomorrow. That's a fact! A basic bibliography for pastors, denominational workers, and laymen should include: Alvin Toffler's *Future Shock* (New York: Random House, 1970); John Gardner's *Self-Renewal* (New York: Harper & Row, 1963); Peter Drucker's *The Age of Discontinuity* (New York: Harper & Row, 1969); and Jacques Ellul's *The Technological Society* (New York: Vintage Books, 1967). These are oriented toward the secular, to be sure, but it is that secular society in which we are called to be salt and light. Lyle Schaller's *The Impact of the Future* (Nashville: Abingdon, 1969) and Larry Richard's *A New Face for the Church* (Grand Rapids: Zondervan, 1971) are almost alone in relating these trends to the Church. We

[2] Alvin Toffler. *Future Shock.* (New York: Random House, 1970).

must know not only where we are headed, but *through what* we are to go as well.

HOLY SPIRIT.   Barth said the doctrine of the Holy Spirit was the one of our immediate future. And he was right. Only the leadership of the Spirit can be adequate in a fluid society. But we must go beyond the idea of the Holy Spirit being a "toy" or a "doctrine." It is true that the emphasis on the Holy Spirit was played down after the excesses of the Great Awakening and the early twentieth century variations of it. Doctrinal battles replaced evangelism for nearly half of this present century, and the emptiness of it produced the vacuum which, in turn, led to the charismatic excesses of the immediate past. For some, the rediscovery of the Holy Spirit has been like "a kid with a new toy." The Holy Spirit has become a churchly plaything. B. A. Sizemore rightly reminds us that the first work of the Spirit is to bring order out of chaos (Gen. 1:1, 2) and not the reverse! The other side of the present temptation will be to become doctrinaire about Him. Yet the Holy Spirit is the only answer to renewal in our time. We are "indwelt" by the Spirit and we can know His fulness, but his fulness is not so much an *experience* as an *equipment* for service. We must learn that God operates at room temperature — not in an icebox or a hothouse.

LARGE CHURCHES.   If for no other reason, economics will force us to forego the luxury of small expensive buildings on small expensive corners for small congregations where "everyone can know each other." The large church has many advantages — in terms of resources in personnel and facilities, broader and better programs, and finances to implement them, children's and youth program possibilities, and trained, specialized staff members. It does lack the close fellowship of the smaller church, however. But, in light of the *mission* of the Church, there is no alternative to the larger church. Social life is a *luxury*, not a *necessity*. This, nevertheless, can be offset by utilizing the small group idea to accomplish the same thing. Clusters by interest, age, or neighborhood could become a part of the congregational structure. Whatever the solution — and a solution must be *created* — the future will dictate fewer and larger churches, geared to minister at maximum efficiency. In the meantime, the consolidation which has been the answer to efficiency at every other level of organizational life just might be the answer for the Church. The one-room schoolhouse is now recognized with nostalgic hindsight for what-it-was-but-could-not-be in our society. The small country church beside it is evidence of our failure to keep pace.

PERSONALITY. Much has been said of the "personality cult" of so much of evangelical life, mostly toward charismatic pastors who build churches around themselves. It is in a sense true that this seldom exists anymore anywhere else but in the Church. Where are the other charismatic personalities today? Hollywood no longer has a Clark Gable — indeed, the awards are going more and more to unknown names. This is true in industry (think of Vanderbilt and Carnegie), in politics (Churchill and FDR), and in the arts. There are no giants anymore; or is it that we have become a race of giants where gianthood is more common? I think the latter is true. But why are giants still visible in the Church? Is it that spiritual giants are rare enough to be readily visible? Or is it that spirituality makes giants more "giant-er" than other areas of life and thought? Whichever the case, it is still true that behind every movement is a man who is a leader among men. When they are raised up by God, they cannot "will" their leadership to any successor because it is not theirs to give. This has been true from the Apostle Paul to Dwight L. Moody. But where churches are *deliberately* built around a personality, it is sin. Better yet, giving one's personality-power to the "equipping ministry," rather than "empire-building," will be a better investment than has ever been true before. The same power can be invested in this new and needed direction. In evangelical circles, this is a must.

PROGRAMS. Where do our church programs come from? They come from the hearts and minds of godly men who are rightly concerned about the things of God. But if we believe that each one has his unique ministry and that each member is brought into the congregation by the Holy Spirit to fulfill a function of the Body, aren't we starting at the wrong end in programing? That is, instead of sitting around thinking up good things to do and then trying to enlist and train people to do them, why not start with the idea that people have ministries which have been given to them by God, and seek to discover, provide training, and offer channels to actualize those ministries? Of course, little would get done that way, but that says more about our lack of spirituality than it does the idea! Yet this is the method most successfully used in small groups. Why not, then, the churches?

RENEWAL. While it was briefly mentioned in Chapter Five, the attempt at the renewal of existing churches, with its often slow pace, has led some to the conclusion that it is a venture beyond hope. The easy solution is to create a new church with no traditions. But this misses the idea of renewal entirely; it is not "renewal," it is simply "new." Who is to blame for those attitudes which hinder, for the smallness of vision, for the sacredness applied to many life-less functions and structures? The truth is, we are! It is like making a mess of one's marriage and thinking the solution is to start another marriage somewhere else with someone else. As Larry Richards says, "We can give no thought to a 'divorce' by reason of incompatibility." [3] Our first obligation in renewal is to the existing church. But two generations of wrong will not be corrected in two years — the normal life span of the present-day pastor. Renewal requires a man pitching his tent for a few years, and it requires a congregation learning to live with "a man sent from God" (who is first *a man*) after the fabled honeymoon is over. Most churches and pastors don't know what to do with each

[3] Richards. *A New Face for the Church*, p. 210.

other after two or three years, mostly because of the mutual discovery of each other's humanity. I have even heard dedicated laymen say that "a change is good, you know; a man can stay too long." I wonder, if a pastor said this to laymen about their jobs, what the reaction would be! Until we learn to actualize the Kingdom by loving "*in spite of*" in our church-pastoral relations, we have little (or nothing) to say to a divided world. "Physician, heal thyself!"

RETREAT HOUSES.   There is a great need today for retreat houses for churches and church groups to use. It is a tragedy that this need has arisen during the "institutional crisis" of most denominations. That is, nearly every denomination is in the process of divesting itself of colleges, seminaries, children's homes, and hospitals. Spiraling costs have simply forced them to do so. When most of these institutions were started, there was a ready-made vacuum for them. Consequently, many were started, perhaps more than was necessary or at least feasible. But, be that as it may, the divesting process is on. Most denominations now view any new institutions as they would a plague. Yet retreat houses are *needed!* This means local churches will have to erect them, perhaps several churches going together to do so.

Houses like Laity Lodge and Yokefellow House are in great demand, and many church groups are forced to use boys and girls camps (YMCA, YWCA, Scouts) which are not really compatible with the purpose of retreats. Beyond the fact that they are usually dormitory style, creating problems for couples, they are frequently "rougher" than most adults prefer. Ideally such lodges should be located near metropolitan areas but isolated enough to be "away." Nature, water, woods, and retreats go together. It should contain rooms with twin beds to accommodate couples or men's or women's groups, and it should contain a large, circular fireside room. Economy suggests that a large lodge able to accommodate two or more groups is good. This means eating together in a central dining hall but meeting in separate wings of the lodge. This is "ideal," however.

Most churches will be forced to seek farmhouses near ponds or waterfront estates. One consideration not yet fully explored is the purchase and conversion of some of the many motels on former major highways, now by-passed by interstate expressways.

VIDEO TAPES. Someday the Church must stop ignoring the fact that television has been invented and that it is limited to commercial efforts. Of great interest and promise is the video tape. Relatively inexpensive and growing more so, the "machines" needed are few and easily maintained. The real challenge, however, will be to produce usable tapes inexpensively and to make them available for rental or for sale without being financially prohibitive. Perhaps the single denomination doing it is not the answer; here is an opportunity for cooperation. A film for training, educating, or inspiring could be jointly produced and marketed, and — if interpretation is needed for a particular group — the denominations could produce sectarian study guides to use with it. One only needs to think of the proliferating possibilities for such, especially with regard to hearing and seeing many of the great spiritual guides of our time — in our own churches. This might also be a challenge (or a ministry) for some Christian in manufacturing: to produce this equipment for churches.

Thus emptieth my bag! These are but ideas struggling to be born. Some of them will be stillbirths, I'm confident, and all of them need refinement. But the future awaits us, a future which will not tolerate yesterday's Church in today's world, let alone the world of tomorrow. Our spirit of adventure, once the hallmark of the God Movement, is sadly wanting. We are afraid of dying and, at the same time, dying of fear. We need holy boldness. Clarence Jordan once parodied our "boldness" in an unforgettable sermon on the children of Israel finding giants in the land. He said:

No doubt these children of Israel tried to justify their fears by having study courses on giants. I imagine that they went to the library and got an encyclopedia down and looked up "giants, species of, life histories of, emotional habits of, effects of giants' heels on grasshoppers." And I think, as a result of that study, they came to the conclusion that they had to be practical. This was a serious matter, and they would have to map out some strategy. So they appointed a social action committee to map the strategy. They came up with the recommendation that they invade this new land with leaflets and that they put on a "Be Kind to Grasshoppers" week. Then, of course, they had to have a finance committee to raise funds for the "Be Kind to Grasshoppers" week, and for the relief of widows of squished grasshoppers. [4]

Yet boldness remains our need as we face the tantalizing future. The future is God's and in His hands. As Vander Warner saw it, we have a choice much like Esau's: whether or not to trade our future for a mess of contemporary pottage.

This is an hour of challenge. And of promise. No one has better expressed it than Moe Hirschberger in Adela Rogers St. John's *Tell No Man,* when he said to Hank Gavin:

"Something's up, young Hank, something's abroad, we're stirring in our long sleep. I'm not an intellectual giant though many of my race are philosophical thinkers of the first water, I'm a pharmacist in a drugstore built on sand, but I have antennae, we all have, we've had to develop them to survive. Something vast and new, as when Moses came down from the mountain." [5]

The choice before the Church — you and me — as we face the future is easily expressed: *Vanguard . . . or . . . Rearguard?* Teilhard de Chardin spoke for me, at least: "Let us unflinchingly join the vanguard of those who are ready to risk the climb to the summit."

[4] Lee, ed. *Op. cit.*

[5] Adela Rogers St. John. *Tell No Man.* (New York: Doubleday, 1966), p. 326.

DISCUSSION QUESTIONS

1. Several group members attempt to identify personally with one of the ideas Dr. Haney has presented and verbalize the idea to the group in their own words.

2. Discuss Elton Trueblood's epigram at the beginning of the chapter.

3. Does the group sense that "something's up" as stated by Moe Hirschberger in *Tell No Man?*

CREATIVE GROUP PROCEDURE

Let each member of a group "add" their own "holy hunch" to the chapter: "If there is one thing I see in the future of Christianity, it is . . ." Be careful to deal with *solutions* as well as *problems*.

THE HERITAGE PLAN

*A Strategy for Establishing Small Groups
in An Existing Congregation*

[*Author's Note:* My original inclination was to include
no report of our small group system at Heritage Church.
I feel very strongly that every church needs the responsibility of following the Spirit's leadership on its own,
and there is no better place to begin than with the development of a program of deepening and widening a
church's life. Mere copying is a shortcut which ultimately short-changes a congregation.

This was offset, however, by two countering reasons.
First, other churches began seeking the counsel of our
experience, and the teams who visited these churches
have all reported that the question they hear is: *how?*
This led me to believe that the method given us might
be a part of our stewardship. Second, when I spoke with
leaders of renewal in my own and other denominations,
they urged the sharing of it most strongly. The value,
they say, is that we were able to "pull it off" in an *existing church.* Most of the successful renewal reports
have come from congregations which started new with
the ideas or those who required or underwent a split
to do it. The great need, they said, was to show how
it can be done within the continuing life of an existing
church.

Thus, I share it. In a very, very real sense, it is not
ours. At the beginning we planned nothing and the
structure grew in response to felt needs. The pattern

which emerged is one we noted only in retrospect; it was not programed in advance. Having "recognized" the pattern, we have been able to follow it successfully in subsequent efforts, but always with an openness toward change. When I shared this with the group involved, they felt the need and desire to share it. This, then, is our "interim report" (the expression we now use instead of "testimony" at Heritage) and a suggested pattern.]

1. *Address the Hunger.* The place to begin is not with a group; it is with the heart. Address the hunger in the hearts of God's people for "the more" which God has and which they know He has, but which they don't have — and know they don't! We used a church-wide Deeper Life Conference with Dr. James Mahoney. (A retreat could also be used.) Following the services each night, any who were interested could go to a home to discuss the message with the speaker. This became the nucleus of our first group. We simply asked if they were interested in further discussion and said that, if so, we could meet later.

2. *Initiate the Group.* We have found that a *monthly* meeting is the best method for an *existing* church. In such a congregation those most interested in the deeper ways of God are already burdened by the program. If the idea is to disciple the church rather than disrupt it, this is an important factor. The name "Yokefellow" was used to identify it, but the usual Yokefellow "minimum discipline" was only encouraged, not required. [1] The group met in a home

---

[1] The "minimum discipline" for Yokefellows is: (1) daily prayer, (2) daily Scripture, (3) weekly fellowship in worship and groups, (4) planned giving to the cause of Christ, (5) unapologetic witness, and (6) study of Christian books. Yokefellow "commitment cards" are available through Yokefellows, 230 College Avenue, Richmond, IN 47374.

It is to be emphasized that Yokefellows is not an organization which anyone can "join"; one "becomes" a Yokefellow as he commits himself to the discipline. As a movement, it does not seek to add any more organizations to the Christian cause; it is to encourage and strengthen existing ones by encouraging a disciplined life. Elton Trueblood, founder of the Yokefellow idea, is fond of saying, "We are not putting another pot on the fire; we are trying to build bigger fires under the existing pots." By providing literature, retreat centers, and resources, Yokefellows seek to be an ally of local churches and groups.

(and this is crucial), *not the church building*. Experience has taught us that one regular home for the meeting is best. The residence of Floyd and Wanda Barker became our meetingplace. A large living or family room, allowing for growth, is good; a fireplace is even better! (The Barkers, we later learned, had already dedicated their home to whatever use the Lord chose! A large yoke hangs over the fireplace now and there is a deep sense of common ownership to the room.)

3. *Focus on Ministry*. The *purpose* of the renewal group is the creation of the ministry idea. Deal constantly with ministry and what it means; and with the ministry of the Holy Spirit. (The author's *Renew My Church* was written to be used by beginning groups to introduce the renewal principles.) Since Bible study is regular fare in most evangelical churches, other books add variety to the approach. Books we have used and found profitable (which is to say we found some others not so profitable) are: Trueblood's *Company of the Committed, The Incendiary Fellowship*, and *The New Man for Our Time;* Keith Miller's *The Taste of New Wine* and *A Second Touch;* Urie Bender's *The Witness;* Ralph Neighbour's *The Touch of the Spirit;* Sam Shoemaker's *Extraordinary Living For Ordinary Men*. Other books on our docket to be used are Bruce Larson's *Dare To Live Now* and *Setting Men Free*. [2] The meeting opens with prayer, the chapter is presented, discussion follows, and then there is a period of fellowship over Coke and coffee to allow for individual conversation.

There will come a time when it dawns on the group what is meant by "ministry." It will come with a breaking, burdening power. Count on it. When it comes, you are underway! Lest anyone misunderstand, this was a four-year period at Heritage. Don't rush or tarry: *wait*.

4. *Conduct a Retreat*. When the group is ready to accept their call to the ministry, they need to (1) study small group dynamics; (2) study the possibilities of groups for

[2] These books are footnoted elsewhere in the book.

growth and service; (3) share felt needs for groups which they see; and (4) pray for God's leadership. A retreat for this *specific* purpose is the best approach. At the next regular meeting, give time for prayer and leadership to take place.

5. *Initiate the Groups.* Many ideas can be suggested by the whole group as to what small groups are possible or needed (Bible study, prayer, tasks, etc.), but the "felt need" is the key. Each will share his felt need; if there is a "match" among them, a small group is under way!

These small groups meet weekly or every other week, with all gathering for the monthly meeting. To distinguish these, we call the monthly assembly a "Yokefellow Group" and the smaller weekly ones "Yoke Groups." Some of the Yoke groups will be long term; others will be short. Let both birth and death be natural. Other groups will change in purpose. For instance, out of our retreat came a group desirous of mutual help in child-rearing. After exhausting their study in six weeks, they elected to stay together as a Bible study group. One sharing group met for a while and died, having served its purpose. No one from the Yoke-fellow group is required to join in the Yoke groups, though most do. Each Yokefellow meeting now begins with "What's going on in the groups?" and any further "felt needs" are requested. If there is a "match," they discuss it during the fellowship period privately. The rule is that these must be Spirit-led and not pastor-programed. This is a risk for any pastor, but it has been greatly lessened by the monthly meetings and understanding of small group dynamics which has preceded it. This is why we urge that this pastor-led preparation period is a must.

Samples of the groups which we have or have had are as follows: a biweekly prayer group on Thursday nights; a weekly Bible study group and a biweekly one; a task group working at the state hospital; a couples sharing group. One of our most exciting is a women's group. One Tuesday morning each month they meet at the church for a secular program to which they can freely invite their friends: How to Decorate Cakes, Sewing, How to Entertain in Your Home. An all-day free nursery is provided so the ladies can go shopping, lunch, get to know the guests. Most times the group breaks up into smaller shopping groups for this. The "hooker" is that the next Tuesday they have a Bible study to which they can invite their friends!

Conversely, the continuing problem and temptation we face is that of growing inward without growing outward. The monthly group is open enough, however, for periodic self-admonishment for this. As the group grows there will be a periodic need to conduct "review" retreats to bring the group together in spiritual maturity.

We have now initiated a group for median-age adults which we call Yokefellow Two. The initial group, now Yokefellow One, started as an all-age group but emerged as a young couples group. We learned: age groups divide themselves as a matter of course and choice. Their needs and their schedules are simply different: children are grown and gone, men are at the management level now in the Two group, whereas nurseries must be provided for the younger couples, the ladies' schedules are governed by the children, and the men are still "climbing" in their employment. (We especially noted this as the Two group studied the same book One had earlier. A chapter on living the Christian life at work resulted in an altogether different set of questions! One wanted to know how to "climb" and be Christian, too, and Two wanted to know how to deal with the "climbers" under them!) Yokefellow Two is still in the monthly-meeting-only stage.

A Yokefellow Three is now in the planning, but with a different goal in mind. Rather than to work toward Yoke groups, it will (hopefully) result in a senior citizens program. It will be initiated as a monthly daytime Bible study.

Altogether, it should result in three Yokefellow "clusters." At present we can diagram it as follows with dotted lines indicating goals. One guiding principle, however, is that goals are always flexible and subject to change.

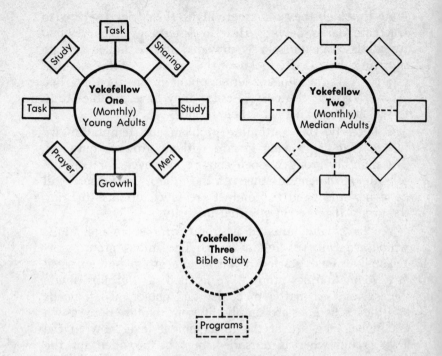

We foresee the eventful need for a quarterly (perhaps) meeting of all the Yokefellow clusters and the possible value of some crossbreeding of the Yoke Groups of One and Two.

6. *Appoint a Coordinator.* With so many groups going, starting, stopping, and with some of the groups "closed" (particularly the short-term sharing groups), a coordinator is required. The responsibility is not to lead or direct, but rather (1) to be apprised when and where the groups are meeting to be able to introduce new people into them and (2) to serve as an ever-reading "resource" person to suggest books and group possibilities. Let the election be a group choice.

7. *Structure it In.* Ultimately, the group structure can be easily added to the existing church structure. Most evangelical congregations have the same basic pattern of church organization. It can be something like the following pattern:

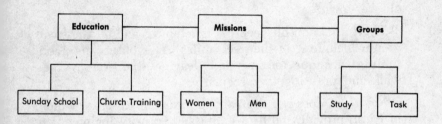

Most churches have some form of the education and missions structures; they can add the other. A possible conflict with the existing men's and women's mission groups with Yoke groups for men or women can be offset by trying to restrict the Yokefellow activities to "couples" and when a men's or women's group needs to be free from the denominational name for evangelistic purposes. We like to say that these are not "church groups"; they are simply groups in which all the members happen to go to the same church! It does point up a challenge for maturity in most churches, however. Existing church groups *can* become jealous and forget that *results* are more important than who gets the credit.

THE VALUE FOR "EXISTING" CHURCHES

The value of the Heritage Plan for *existing* churches is fourfold.

First, the pastor is integrally involved and can guide the group in the monthly meeting. The great fear of pastors (warranted in many cases) is that groups will "get away" from the church, and this solves the problem.

Second, it is a part of the program, not parallel with it. One of the questions most often asked our teams which go to other churches on request is: "What does this do to the *program?*" We find our Yokefellows are usually the most involved in both! The only program we have seen adversely affected is Wednesday night "prayer meeting," since many of those who would otherwise attend are in other groups during the week. However, we see this as "prayer-meeting-all-over-town."

Third, the monthly meeting is retained, and all the small groups include it in their schedules. This offsets the possibility of a clique forming and "leaving" the group. They walk and pray together regularly.

Fourth, it does not supplant the existing structure which, in truth, provides both meaning and security for members not inclined toward the groups; it also keeps the group members involved in the regular programs. Thus the entire church is interrelated through the existing programs of worship and Bible study.

SMALL GROUP EVALUATION SHEET *

This is a sample evaluation sheet for use in a variety of small group meetings. It may be copied or adapted without further permission. Group members should simply be instructed to give their honest and immediate impressions in response to the following questions.

IN THIS MEETING   (Circle one category for each statement)

1. LEADERSHIP WAS	Dominated by one person	Dominated by a subgroup	Centered in about half the group	Shared by all members of the group
2. COMMUNICATION WAS	Badly blocked	Difficult	Fairly open	Very open and free-flowing
3. PEOPLE WERE	Phony	Hidden	Fairly open	Honest and authentic
4. THE GROUP WAS	Avoiding its task	Loafing	Getting some work done	Working hard at its task
5. I FELT	Misunderstood and rejected	Somewhat misunderstood	Somewhat accepted	Completely accepted and understood by the group

6. The one word I would use to describe the climate of the meeting: _____

7. Suggestions:

* Clyde Reid. *Groups Alive — Church Alive*, p. 60.

Appendix C

The following books are suggested for discovering the various possibilities and styles of retreats.

Father Andrew. *In the Silence.* London: Mowbray, 1948.

Carpenter-Garnier, Mark. *Retreats and How to Conduct Them.* London: The Pax House, 1930.

Casteel, John L. *Renewal Through Retreats.* New York: Association Press, 1957.

Haney, David P. *Renew My Church.* Grand Rapids: Zondervan, 1972. pp. 74-75.

Living My Religion on My Job. New York: The Laymen's Movement, 1962.

Nelson, John Oliver. *Retreats for Protestants.* Bangor, Pa.: Kirkridge. Pamphlet.

Planning a Retreat. Rock Island, Ill.: Lutheran Board of Publication. Pamphlet.

Richards, Lawrence O. *A New Face For the Church.* Grand Rapids: Zondervan, 1971. pp. 167f.

Steere, Douglas V. *Time to Spare.* New York: Harper & Row, 1949.

Wareham, James. *The Conducting of Retreats.* London: Mowbray, 1950.

Appendix D

The following Litany of Dedication reflects the "dedicated for" idea. It was used by Heritage Baptist Church for its Dedication Service on March 5, 1972. (The State of Maryland purchased the former College Avenue property and the Church was able to construct a $1,015,000 building on a new 10-acre site debt-free.) Note in particular the *purposes* for which the building was dedicated.

The Litany of Dedication

As a MEETINGHOUSE for the study and the proclamation of the Word to children and youth, to collegians and midshipmen, to adults and families . . .

PEOPLE: We dedicate this House.

As a HEADQUARTERS for the company of believers, known collectively as the Heritage Baptist Church, and from which the gathered group shall scatter to become as holy seed in the Annapolis fields . . .

PEOPLE: We dedicate this House.

As a MEMORIAL to our College Avenue past, acknowledging our debt to a great cloud of witnesses now above us, and yet in spirit with us . . .

PEOPLE: We dedicate this House.

As a SERVICE CENTER to our community, providing a place of refreshment for the bodies, minds and spirits of those to whom it is our responsible privilege to minister in the name of Christ our Lord . . .

PEOPLE: We dedicate this House.

As a SANCTUARY, a place where prayer is wont to be made, baptisms and communion observed, tithes and offerings given, hymns sung and anthems heard, a place where we our Savior meet . . .

PEOPLE: We dedicate this House.

In the NAME of, and for the GLORY of, and by the GRACE of God the Father, God the Son, and God the Holy Spirit . . .

PEOPLE: We dedicate this House. ©